Dorset & Somerset
Edited by Angela Fairbrace

First published in Great Britain in 2008 by:
Young Writers
Remus House
Coltsfoot Drive
Peterborough
PE2 9JX
Telephone: 01733 890066
Website: www.youngwriters.co.uk

All Rights Reserved

© Copyright Contributors 2008

SB ISBN 978-1 84431 673 1

Foreword

Young Writers was established in 1991 and has been passionately devoted to the promotion of reading and writing in children and young adults ever since. The quest continues today. Young Writers remains as committed to the nurturing of poetic and literary talent as ever.

This year's Young Writers competition has proven as vibrant and dynamic as ever and we are delighted to present a showcase of the best poetry from across the UK and in some cases overseas. Each poem has been selected from a wealth of *Little Laureates 2008* entries before ultimately being published in this, our seventeenth primary school poetry series.

Once again, we have been supremely impressed by the overall quality of the entries we have received. The imagination, energy and creativity which has gone into each young writer's entry made choosing the poems a challenging and often difficult but ultimately hugely rewarding task - the general high standard of the work submitted ensured this opportunity to bring their poetry to a larger appreciative audience.

We sincerely hope you are pleased with this final collection and that you will enjoy *Little Laureates 2008 Dorset & Somerset* for many years to come.

Contents

Sami Kumaila (9) — 1

Archbishop Wake Primary School, Blandford
Paige Smith (10) — 2
Sophie Babbs (11) — 3
Callum Wray (9) — 4
Miguel Bernabéu (10) — 5
Connor Rosoman (10) — 6
Harun Cakir (11) — 6
Amy Lillywhite (10) — 7
Oliver Hooper (10) — 7
Billy Bailey (9) — 8
Jack Lane (11) — 8
Liam Gonthier (10) — 9
Max Frampton (9) — 9
Olie Taylor (11) — 10
Ruby Bircham (10) — 11
Jack Pennick (9) — 12

Binegar CE (VC) Primary School, Binegar
Alec Southwell (8) — 12
Daisy Bown (9) — 13
Elly Hayman (7) — 13
Chantelle Wilkins (9) — 14
Kyle Seago (9) — 14

Castle Court School, Wimborne
Jamie Wheeler (10) — 15
Ellie Friend (10) — 15
Jasmin Bourton (11) — 16
Nicholas Morris (11) — 16
Jessica Chipperdale (11) — 17
Dominic Jones (11) — 17
Harvey Wingfield (11) — 18
Georgia Byrne (10) — 19
George Nix (11) — 20
Joshua Daplyn (9) — 20

Bethany Holmes (11)	21
Kathleen Rafferty (11)	21
Charlie Parry (10)	22
Anna Powell (10)	22
Oliver Alder (10)	23
Joe Payne (11)	23
Annabel Boothright (10)	24
Will Hosford (11)	24
Harry Middleton (10)	25
Edward Southgate (9)	25
Maxwell Noble (9)	26
Harry Wheildon (9)	26
Annabel Snook (9)	27
Arthur Bowden (10)	27
Tim Rutland (9)	28
Jack James Martin (9)	29
Harry Agombar (9)	30
Georgina Tucker (9)	30
Rosie Hellewell (9)	31
Samuel Wheeler (9)	31
Henry Imms (9)	32
Harrison Jones (8)	33
Toby Woodhouse (9)	34
Benjamin Battey (9)	35
Luke Robinson (8)	36
Felix Scull (9)	36
Rupert Peter Ward Bennett (9)	37
Oliver Jessup (8)	37
Georgina Carter (9)	38
Alexandra Sanders (8)	38
Tommy Bridger (8)	39
Henry Baugniet (9)	39
William Jacobs (8)	40
Luciano De Bacci (8)	40
Alfred Streeton (9)	41
Alastair Carter (9)	41
Edward Southgate (8)	42
Kyle Flower (9)	42
Rosie Southgate (7)	43
Lucy Chapple (8)	43
Chris Rutland (8)	44
Nicola Nuttall (8)	44

Tom Tombs (9)	45
Megan Griffiths (9)	45
Thomas Powell (9)	46
Oliver Groat (8)	47
Rosie Alder (9)	48
Harrison Faull (8)	49
Leo Pembroke (8)	50
Maia Knowles (8)	51
Henry Halewood (9)	52
Arthur Cordwell (8)	52
Oliver Jones (10)	53
Alex Waller-Edwards (11)	53
Thomas Erbetta (10)	54
Giovanni De Bacci (10)	54
Bryony Bennett (11)	55
Daisy Poole (11)	55
Tamar Tucker-Harrison (10)	56
Louisa De Paola (10)	56
Oscar Brooks (9)	57
Alex Schuster-Bruce (10)	57
George Acworth (10)	58
Alistair Warr (9)	59
Sebastian Fletcher (9)	60
Alexander Stocks (9)	61
Harry Schotel (10)	62
Ella Clayton (9)	63
Victoria Webb (9)	64
James Mullins (11)	65

Chewton Mendip CE (VA) School, Chewton Mendip

Badger Class	66

Corpus Christi Catholic Primary School, Boscombe

Tayla Carlsson (9)	67
Connor Rowlett (9)	68
Aleasha Mallon (9)	68
Kara Abbott (10)	69
Mary Roughley (9)	69
Leila Dixon (9)	70
Nadine Barber (10)	70
Jack Figg (9)	70

Daniel Hawkins (10) 71
Gaby Smith (9) 71
Jamie Wilkinson (9) 71
Connor Trussell (9) 72
Nicole Livesey (9) 72

Court De Wyck Primary School, Claverham
Samuel Maddix (10) 73
Jack Drake (11) 73
Lizzy Maddix (9) 74
Martin Segers (10) 74
Harvey Pearson (9) 74
Elisabeth Hunt (10) 75
Zack Tinkling (11) 75
Chelsea Heal (9) 75
Sophie Cepek (9) 76
Holly Hancock (10) 76
Lewis Drake (9) 76
Andrew Gray (10) 77
Lauren Victoria Blewett (10) 77
Daniel Summers Singleton (9) 77
Maisie E Workman (9) 78
Bailey Thomas (10) 78
India McKeown (9) 78
Shane Bellotti (11) 79
Amberleigh Gallichan (11) 79

Crockerne CE (VC) Primary School, Pill
Thomas Mitchell (8) 79
Lili Harvey (8) 80
Francesca May Hollis (7) 80
Sophie Hutchings (8) 80
Ryan Croker (8) 81
Tanya Hanlon (8) 81
Lucy Mayer (8) 81
Alexander Leakey (9) 82
Megan Birch Morgan (9) 82
Eloise Wheeler (8) 82
Natasha Brooks (11) 83
Jack Sharp (10) 83
Phoebe Sherborne (10) 84

Jack Parslow (10)	85
Grace Arnall (11)	86
Angus Mason (7)	86
James Smith (11)	87
Bethany Taylor (9)	87
Rosey Skilbeck (10	88
Connie Mansfield (10)	88
Jay Webber-Andrews (10)	89
Emma Gould (9)	89
Robyn Byrne (9)	90
Oliver James Gedge (9)	91
Ava Parry (9)	92
Sophie Cashman (10)	93
Jake Mobbs (10)	94

Horsington CE Primary School, Horsington

Tom Bullen (7)	94
Katy Rumbelow (9)	95
Phoebe Morris (7)	95
Matthew Salthouse (9)	96
Jessica Brewer (8)	96
Ellie Martin (9)	97
Olivia Wingate (7)	97
Sophie Maunsell (8)	98
Rebecca Croxton (8)	98
James Dighton (7)	99
Alfie Jones (8)	99
Alice Jackson (9)	100
Toby Crabb (8)	100
Siobhán Reynolds (8)	101
Amelia Tarling (8)	101
Alice Liddle (7)	102
Kate Homer (9)	102
Megan Terry (8)	103
Jasmine Hooper (8)	103
Francesca Wagstaff (8)	104
Sián Charlotte Reynolds (8)	104
Harry Carnell (9)	105

Kilmersdon CE (VA) Primary School, Kilmersdon
Daniel Powney (10)   105
Millie Bishop (8)   106
Rachel Ayles (9)   106
Faris Ravetta (8)   106
Regan Downing (9)   107
Ben Watts-Hewson (10)   107
Sam Watts (8)   107
Emily Boyd-Nash (9)   108
Georgia Pielesz (8)   108
Dexter Brodrick (9)   108
Jack Parsons (9)   109
Richard Bowker (8)   109
Bonnie Weeks (10)   109
Billy Seymour (9)   110
Sebastian Roberts (10)   110
Jacob Williams (9)   110
Georgia Hughes (8)   111
Josiah Bond (10)   111
Rowan Read (9)   111
Sam Woodruff (9)   112

Oldfield Park Junior School, Bath
Charley Buchan (8)   112
Brooklyn Ashdown-Doel (8)   113
Daniel Clausen (10)   113
Toby Fielding (10)   114
Tom Matthews (9)   114
Jasmine Jade Knight (8)   115
Tom Whittaker (9)   115
Evie Hillier (8)   116
Maisey Sprake (7)   116
Alexis McLeod (10)   116
Ruthie Marshall (7)   117
Megan Fortune (8)   117
Hamish James Kale (9)   118

Puriton Primary School, Puriton
Jadene Gardener & Sophie Milsom (11)   118
Elspeth Megan MacGeoch & Jordan Palmer (9)   119
Ellie Lay & Hannah Hughes (10)   119

Sam Umimski (10) & Thomas Lonsdale (11)	120
Asher Bentham (11)	120
Matthew Betteridge, Connor Wolfe-Middleton, Charlie Attwood & William Lonsdale	121
Melissa Standen & Leah Beechey (10)	121
Georgia Edmundson, Leah Turner & Tanisha Birch (11)	122
Lucy Russell, Melissa Storey, Sophie Hembery & Holly Cartright-Hall	123
Anthony Lawson-Blake, Liam Chinn, Connor Ferris & Joe Dixon	124
Niamh McKay (11)	125
Amber Howden (10)	126

Sandford Primary School, Sandford

Kieran James Woodhouse (10)	127
Jamie O'Connor	128
Adam Karl Nichols (10)	128
Gregory Humphry (8)	129
Libby Wilsher-Day (8)	129
Megan Pressling (8)	130
Dominic Thorne (11)	131
Adam Jones (11)	132
Holly Bartholomew (9)	132
Greta Guccione (9)	133
Matthew Callow (9)	133
Chloe James (11)	134
Jack Hill (7)	135
Georgina Staite (10)	136
Georgia Douglas (8)	137
Amy Lees (9)	138

Sticklands CE (VA) Primary School, Evershot

Francesca Farquharson (7)	138
Charlie Oldfield (9)	139
Alice Glover (7)	139
Alice Crocker (8)	140
Hamish Moore (8)	140
Chloe Diment (7)	141
Scout MacPherson (8)	141
Tara Newman (8)	142
Nathaniel Anstey (8)	142

Elizabeth Crocker (9) — 142
Theodora Cottrell (7) — 143
Callum Symes (8) — 143
Ellie Robins (8) — 143
Samie Gough (9) — 144
Rebecca Glover (7) — 144
Toby Dolan (8) — 144
Alexandra Adams (8) — 145
Isobel Farquharson (9) — 145
Lola Francis (9) — 145
Esme Diment (9) — 146
Eilah Berlow (9) — 146
Adam Harris (8) — 147
Corey Brimble (7) — 147
Jack Ruston (7) — 148
Imogen Bellfield (7) — 148

Woolavington Village Primary School, Woolavington
Melanie Russon (8) — 148
Abbie Fisher (8) — 149
Tom Kidner (8) — 149
Chloe Louise Chick (7) — 149
Katie Goldrich (9) — 150
Kieran Long (8) — 150
Jack Willis (8) — 151
Joshua Foale (8) — 151
Thomas Puddy (9) — 152
Jaime Farrell (9) — 152
Katie Crossman (9) — 153
Emma Howes (8) — 153
Charly Moore (9) — 154
Lucy Pacey (8) — 154
Caitlin Pinney (9) — 155
Samuel Bate (8) — 155
Henry Isaacs (8) — 156
Kayla Rossiter (8) — 156

The Poems

What I Celebrate

I celebrate
The sight of the sun
Blazing across the world
And the clouds shooting through the sky.

I celebrate
The sound of rustling trees
Shaking in the wind.

I celebrate
The feel of the shower
Trickling down my body.

I celebrate
The taste of sweet things
Munching in my mouth
And running down my throat.

I celebrate
The memory of when I got my DS
When I was very ill in France.

I celebrate
The colour of blue paint
Sliding down my page
And light blue swiping from my brush.

Sami Kumaila (9)

The Enormous Elephant

The enormous elephant
Is as big as ten double-decker buses
And as grey as a stormcloud ready to burst.

The enormous elephant
Has four stamping feet
As big as houses
And is as grey as a dusty old book.

The enormous elephant
Loves walking around, making the ground shake
And likes squirting water out of its trunk.

The enormous elephant
Has a tail as big as a skyscraper,
That brushes against the floor.

The enormous elephant
Has two big eyes as huge as beach balls,
Looking at you all the time.

The enormous elephant
Has two big ears,
Like amazing long plane wings,
Swooping along in the breezy air.

That's my enormous elephant!

Paige Smith (10)
Archbishop Wake Primary School, Blandford

Rainstorm

Rain,
You who swoops down,
Flying across the sky,
Flashing your golden wings,
Have you come in anger?

Rain,
You who charges through the sky,
Feet pounding like a drum,
Running across the sky,
Why do you come?

Rain,
You who slithers through the sky,
Destroying things in your way,
But being so silent,
Are you here to help?

Rain,
You who flies down from above,
Attacking your prey,
At every chance you have,
Why are you so strong?

Rain,
You who are so huge
Splashing your breath across the sky,
Your breath pounding on the ground,
Thank you for a rainstorm.

Sophie Babbs (11)
Archbishop Wake Primary School, Blandford

The Pouncing Puma

My puma's coat is a black cloud,
Floating in the sky.
It's like a feather, shimmering up high.
His fur is polished diamond,
Lighting up a huge museum.

His teeth are like hundreds of pickaxes,
Digging into a wall,
Like a chugging chainsaw cutting through a tree.

His claws are severely sharp saws,
Shimmering in the sun,
Like a vampire's canines, biting his prey.

When he bellows,
He sounds as beautiful as a bird,
On a hot summer's day.

When he runs he is like an F1 racing car,
Speeding around the track,
Like a rocket shooting up into space.

His eyes light up all the dark rooms,
They are like stars across the night sky.

His sense of smell is great when he hunts his prey.
If his prey were a million miles away,
He will catch it within one day.

Callum Wray (9)
Archbishop Wake Primary School, Blandford

African Rainstorm

Rain!
You, who makes a tune,
Drumming throughout the land,
Making yourself heard,
Anywhere you go,
Why are you here?

Rain!
You, who brings friends of thunder and lightning,
A rampaging rhino running into the ground,
And a charging elephant racing through the clouds,
Taking it in turns to do what you do,
Have your friends come in peace?

Rain!
You, who is hidden by a cloud,
Millions of giant hippos
Moving slowly along
In a single line,
Will you stop when it gets too much?

Rain!
You, who can be defeated by just one thing,
The wind, a howling wolf
Who can blow you away,
Or blow us apart,
Are you friend or foe?

Rain!
You can be good to us,
Or you can be bad,
You, who brings friends for us,
A team you are,
Are you our friend or not?

Miguel Bernabéu (10)
Archbishop Wake Primary School, Blandford

Rain

Rain
As if a herd of antelope storm the savannah,
You create huge dust clouds,
A rain cloud emerges.
Will you be kind?
Because then we won't mind.

Rain
As you howl like a wolf,
Our trees collapse.
You can fill a balloon,
But why do we get this misfortune?

Rain
You spit and bully,
Why have you betrayed us?
As a rattlesnake hisses.
You hurl us your disses.

Rain
The monstrous flash fills the sky,
The lightning makes the children cry,
As agile serpent pounces,
You light the town and you can fly.

Connor Rosoman (10)
Archbishop Wake Primary School, Blandford

Rampaging Rhino

Mr Rhino is fast, like a blazing wind.
Grey skin, like a dark, rainy day.
Soft skin, like a piece of soft leather.
Teeth like a sharp fork.
His horn is like a ten ton truck.
Claws like a heavyweight.
His golden white teeth like a piece a chewing gum.
Beautiful shining skin, like a sparkly mirror.

Harun Cakir (11)
Archbishop Wake Primary School, Blandford

My Super, Secret Pet

His roar is as talented as Leona Lewis,
His teeth are as sharp as a horrible hedge cutter,
His fur is as soft as a beautiful baby's bottom,
His mane is as wild as my hair on a magnificent morning,
His claws are as violent as a galloping gunner.
He is as strong as lightning, zooming down from above, sharply.
He leaps around, trying to catch his prey.

What is my super, secret pet?

Amy Lillywhite (10)
Archbishop Wake Primary School, Blandford

Rain

Rain!
You who come all of a sudden,
Extraordinary, racing down the sky,
Paws pounding in the sky.
Have you come in anger?

Rain!
You blow things away,
Amazingly flapping your wings,
You swing down with a gust of cold air.
Have you come to wash us away?

Rain!
You roar as your great paws crash in the sky,
You scare us and shake us up.
Oh, why do you do this?
Have you come to attack us?

Rain!
You who gather in the sky,
You cover it like the night sky,
You roll in, coveting excellent sky.
Have you come to ruin our blue sky?

Oliver Hooper (10)
Archbishop Wake Primary School, Blandford

Rain Poem

Rain!
You sound like a giraffe, ripping leaves off a high tree,
And you sound like a shaker on the rooftops.
Could you play a good tune for all of us?

Rain!
You sound like a giraffe, biting to get the leaves
That is another overgrown giraffe,
Trying to get the leaves from the top of the cracked branch.

Thunder!
You are like an elephant, crashing through the forest
And pounding on the trees
With your mighty feet.

Lightning!
You are like a silver eagle,
Speeding through the air,
Setting fire as you go.

Billy Bailey (9)
Archbishop Wake Primary School, Blandford

The Unpleasant, Magnificent Tiger

My tiger's fur is as comfortable as a cow rug,
His eyes are as bright as a human torch.
His magnificent roar is like an unpleasant tummy rumble.
His teeth are as sharp as a razor blade,
The claws are as powerful as a wasp sting.
My tiger is orange like an African sunset.
Orange, like the blinding, shimmering sun across the plains of Africa.

Jack Lane (11)
Archbishop Wake Primary School, Blandford

He Who Fell Upon Us

Rain!
You, who came down swiftly,
Storming through the sky,
Pushing and stomping clouds of fear.
Have you come in rage?

Rain!
You, who came down swiftly,
Soaring to the ground,
Suddenly appearing to all eyes
And then vanishing without a trace.
Have you come in fear?

Rain!
You who come down swiftly,
Thank you rain for travelling down.

Liam Gonthier (10)
Archbishop Wake Primary School, Blandford

A Shining Lion

My lion is magnificent.
He hunts like a human with spears
But he's better than that.
He swoops over the ground like a hawk
Looking for food.

He succeeds, mostly every time.
He has claws as sharp as a dagger,
Fur as smooth as a fur cushion
And a magnificent mane,
Rough as a broomstick
And his roar is like thunder.
Teeth as sharp as a great white shark.

Max Frampton (9)
Archbishop Wake Primary School, Blandford

Rain

Rain!
Like a crowd of tribesmen beating their drums to the gods,
You charge through the deserted wilderness of the Sahara.
Baring your horns to any passing straggler,
Whilst you and your herd crash and bang your way
through where trees exist.
Kicking up clouds of dust and shrivelled vegetation,
Ruining crops the farmers tried so hard to grow.
Then, all of a sudden, you are gone
And the pounding and drumming of your hooves dies away
Into the distant hills and valleys.
The dust settles back
and the farmers enjoy what you have given them,
Hope,
Hope,
And when you leave you have laid upon this land
a very different scene,
Once beautiful,
Once bursting with life,
Now bare
And laden with dread.

Olie Taylor (11)
Archbishop Wake Primary School, Blandford

Rain

Rain!
You who moans as you race through the cloud
And jump through the clouds
On this wintry night.
Have you come in anger?

Rain!
You who charges across the sky,
Destroying your path in front,
Flashing with your every chance,
Watching us suffer.
Why do you come in such rage?

Rain!
You who speeds across the valley,
Raging towards the end,
But trying to catch your breath,
Still silent in your devious ways.
Do you bring us help?

Rain!
You who rattles rapidly,
Waiting for the world to hear,
Until you pounce upon your prey.
You worry us, but
Thank you, oh mighty rain!

Ruby Bircham (10)
Archbishop Wake Primary School, Blandford

Extraordinary Giraffe

My giraffe is as tall as a tree.
His neck is a ladder, reaching high into the trees.
His eyes are like a telescope.
His legs are as long as two tables.
His tongue is as long as a piece of string ,
reaching for all the fruit and leaves.
His spots are like millions of Smarties.
My giraffe is the best giraffe in the world.

Jack Pennick (9)
Archbishop Wake Primary School, Blandford

Childhood Tracks

Eating spaghetti from a plate as hard as steel.
Eating some chocolate from a bar made of foil
and as brown as a dog's fur.
Eating sweets from a bag.
Eating a plate of chicken made by Mum.
Eating a big apple while watching TV.
Drinking a can of cola.
Drinking milk, as cold as a winter evening.

Hearing a passing car revving its engine like the wind.
Hearing my dog barking at a cat.
Hearing the oven beeping non-stop.
Hearing the bath running and my sister moaning.

Seeing my dog barking like the wind.
Seeing and smelling a stinky bin.
Seeing clouds that look like familiar faces.
Seeing my dad's bedroom, as clean as a diamond.
Seeing my favourite food on a plate.

Smelling apple pie, as hot as the sun.
Smelling a dog from my neighbour's house.
Smelling my mum's perfume, as smelly as a flower.
Smelling tea and cakes in the living room.

Alec Southwell (8)
Binegar CE (VC) Primary School, Binegar

Childhood Tracks

Eating bright orange carrot sticks, with juice running down your chin.
Eating spaghetti with the sauce flicking back onto your cheeks.
Eating tomato soup, steaming hot, slurping it all in before it gets cold.
Eating potatoes with the butter running down them.
Eating chocolate, melting in the top of your mouth, then licking it off.
Eating mashed potato, creamy and as light as a feather.

Hearing the radio on a Saturday morning, telling you what the weather
is going to be.
Hearing dogs barking at nothing but a bumblebee on a summer day.
Hearing the gentle clock ticking every second to tell you the time.
Hearing the washing machine as it goes round at 100 miles per hour.
Hearing the shower as the water drips down and down.
Hearing the Hoover as it hoovers up all the breadcrumbs
that are in sight.

Smelling the roast dinner cooking and the vegetables cooking
until they are tender.
Smelling the lawn cuttings on a summer's day.
Smelling the £20 perfume that smells as nice as a chocolate shop.
Smelling the lavender washing powder everywhere you walk.

Seeing the misted fields in the distance, up on top of a hill.
Seeing the sheep crossing the quiet lane with no one there.
Seeing the hens pecking for a short blade of grass in the sun.
Seeing the farmers harvesting the maize on a bumpy hill.

Daisy Bown (9)
Binegar CE (VC) Primary School, Binegar

Blowing The Candles Out

Blowing the candles out on my birthday,
after just listening to my friends singing *happy birthday* to me
blowing the candles out on my colourful, bright cake.
After I blow out the candles we will shout out,
'I am 8, I am 8!'

Elly Hayman (7)
Binegar CE (VC) Primary School, Binegar

Home

Watching TV.
Bright colours on black screen, it's reflecting my pale face.
Going to bed, dropping my warm head on the light pillow.
Feeling the warmth of the quilt cover.
The swishing noises of the wind, swirling round,
opening my bedroom window,
it blows through the warmth of the room.
Putting on make-up before I lie down,
the blusher blows into my delicate eyes.
With the sun going down on me,
it is like the trees are looking at me down below.
The sky is dull and the moon is coming up
and I am starting to drift off to sleep . . .

Chantelle Wilkins (9)
Binegar CE (VC) Primary School, Binegar

Holiday

Wake up one Friday morning,
Think it's another boring day,
But then I remember . . .
We're going on holiday today.

Go to school, all excited and happy,
Then it's break time, but not in a hurry,
Here comes lunch, nearly there,
Cos we're going on holiday today.

All having fun on the last day of term,
They're all excited because it's the last day,
But not as excited as *me!*
Cos we're going on holiday today.

Kyle Seago (9)
Binegar CE (VC) Primary School, Binegar

The Colour Of My Thoughts

Grey is the stormy sea, angry and violent.
The monster's raging, scarlet eye.
Icy blue is the colour of a lonely child, searching for its mother.
Green is the colour of envy, looking for more and more and revenge.
Black is how I feel when someone close has died.
Yellow is a field of flowers, dancing in the breeze.
Ruby is the colour of wisdom and knowledge kept quiet.
Copper is a coin not yet discovered.
Purple is the coloured background of my dreams.
White is clouds, billowing in the wind.
Lime is the last page of my book, one word from completion.
These are the colours of my thoughts.

Jamie Wheeler (10)
Castle Court School, Wimborne

Colourful Fruits

Green is the colour of a Brussels sprout
Give me one and I'd spit it out.

Purple is the colour of a juicy grape,
Eat 200, then I'll gape.

Red is the colour of a fresh strawberry,
It's even bigger than a cherry.

Orange is a colour and the fruit's the same,
Sometimes peeling can be a pain.

Ellie Friend (10)
Castle Court School, Wimborne

The Poem Of The Rainbow

Red is the colour of the dragon's eye,
Red is the colour of a sunset sky.

Orange is the colour of autumn leaves,
Orange is the colour of the morning breeze.

Green is the colour of a fresh summer's day,
Green is the colour of the environment today.

Blue is the colour of the midsummer sky,
Blue is the colour of my little eye.

Indigo is the colour of my throbbing thumb,
Indigo is the colour of a ripe plum.

Violet is the colour of the flowers in spring,
Violet is the colour of a dragonfly's wing.

Jasmin Bourton (11)
Castle Court School, Wimborne

The Colours Of My World

In my world the rabbits are blue
And green, green grass is red,
All the flowers are white
And all the people are orange and green.
They would give all of you such a big fright.

In my world the sky is purple,
The sand is pink and the crabs are aquamarine.
These are the colours of my world,
The things only I have seen!

Nicholas Morris (11)
Castle Court School, Wimborne

The Colours Of The Rainbow

Red is the colour of a dragon's eye
And the colour of a sunset sky.

Orange is the colour of a ginger fringe
And the colour that makes you cringe.

Yellow is the colour of a rose
And the colour of pus-filled toes.

Green is the colour of the grass
And the colour that makes you laugh.

Blue is the colour of a mermaid's eye
And the colour of a beautiful sky.

Violet is the colour of trees,
As they wave in the twilight breeze.

Indigo is the colour of space
And the colour at the end of a race.

Jessica Chipperdale (11)
Castle Court School, Wimborne

Colours

Red is the colour of a dragon breathing fire.
Blue is the smell of blueberries and a cloudless sky.
Orange is the colour of the sun shining down.
Purple is the colour of a fig.
Grey is the colour of dust and smoke.
Brown is the colour of muddy puddles.
Pink is the smell of strawberries falling.
Green is the colour of leaves on the tree.
Black is the taste of Guinness.

Dominic Jones (11)
Castle Court School, Wimborne

Colours Of My Emotions

Red is thecolour of fire and anger,
It's danger, it's passion, it's Chritmassy fun,
It's the dying embers of a bonfire.

Orange is the colour of the rising sun,
It's a refreshing drink after an August run,
It's funky, it's fruity,
It's the colour of having fun.

Green is the colour of damp, slimy moss,
It's seaweed, helpful traffic lights,
It's the spiky cuttings of freshly mown grass.

Blue is the colour of sweet blueberries,
It's sadness, it's deep, undiscovered seas, days all alone,
It's staring up at a cloudless sky.

Indigo is the colour of the night sky,
It's inky, it's an enchanted wizard's hat,
It's the shade of the jeans I want to buy.

Violet is the colour of a soft, ripe plum,
It's a delicate flower in bud, it's a tender bruise on my thigh,
It's a dusky summer evening I spent having fun.

Harvey Wingfield (11)
Castle Court School, Wimborne

Black And Green

Black
Black is the colour of a moonless night,
The colour of sorrow exhibited at a funeral.
The colour of blankness in a person's eyes.
Black is what lies beneath the deep ocean,
The colour the blind will always see.
Black is the colour of emptiness,
Sometimes found inside you and me.
It is the Angel of Death, as he knocks at your door.
Black is the colour of everyone's weakness.

Green
Green is the colour of my favourite jelly bean,
The colour of the treetops.
Green is an emerald that glows on the ground,
The colour of a camouflaged lizard in the grass.
Green is the colour I feel as I ride in my boat,
The colour of my little brother's T-shirt,
The colour of my new ten-speed bike.
Green is the colour of a microchip in a computer,
The colour of slime at the bottom of a lake.

Georgia Byrne (10)
Castle Court School, Wimborne

The Colours Of England

Bronze is Big Ben, tall and strong,
Emerald is the countryside,
Sapphire is the Thames,
Ruby are the jewels on the royal crown,
Grey are the planes that fly across the sky,
Roses are the flowers that grow at Durlston Park,
White are our rugby shirts,
Red is our flag,
Green is the grass that grows in Hyde Park,
Cream is the colour of the beaches in the south,
Black are the cabs that drive around England,
Scarlet is the colour of the old London phone boxes,
The coat of Nelson was blue,
Yellow are the lights that envelop Tower Bridge,
Crimson are the coats of the changing guard.

George Nix (11)
Castle Court School, Wimborne

Trees

A tree, a beautiful tree,
Twisting and curving elegantly.
Towering above everything else,
Up, up, up higher than all the others.

Trees are slim, wide and huge,
Blinding to the human eye
With beautifulness.

Trees give us fantastic fruits,
Golden pears, crispy apples and more . . .
And in spring they make lots of
Flowers!

Joshua Daplyn (9)
Castle Court School, Wimborne

Colour Poem

Emerald is the colour of the growing leaves,
Emerald is the colour of the murky seas,
Emerald is the colour of an eagle's eye,
Emerald is the colour of a witch's sigh.

Amber is the colour of fierce and wild,
Amber is the colour of warm and mild,
Amber is the colour of a friend's hello,
Amber is the colour of the sunset's glow.

Blue is the colour of forget-me-nots,
Blue is the colour of friendship knots,
Blue is the colour of cold and frost,
Blue is the colour of loved and lost.

Bethany Holmes (11)
Castle Court School, Wimborne

Sapphire

Sapphire is the colour of the dragon's eye
Sapphire is the colour of the midsummer sky
Sapphire is the colour of the calm, calm seas
Sapphire is the colour of the winter trees

Sapphire is a twinkling gemstone
Sapphire is the jewel on an emperor's throne
Sapphire is the princess at the ball
Sapphire is the fairest of them all.

Kathleen Rafferty (11)
Castle Court School, Wimborne

Seasons Of Trees

In autumn the trees are flame-red, scarlet, crimson
The trees are stunning in autumn for they are huge
They feel jagged, rough, bumpy.

In spring and summer the trees' leaves are jade,
　　　　　　emerald, bottle-green, sea-green.
They grow apples, bananas, peaches, kiwis.
They provide shelter for birds, insects and many more.

In winter trees turn pearly with all the snow
The silver frost makes the trees cold
The trees lose all their leaves
The colour turns to its boring winter self again.

Charlie Parry (10)
Castle Court School, Wimborne

Blue

Poisoned pools, depressing deaths,
Cold winter's freezing breaths,
Prussian is like an empty, black hole,
A dark, scary, dead soul.
Indigo is the colour of an eastern bird's head,
Under the sea, where I dread.
Aquamarine is the wave's sigh,
The cries of a guilty person's lie.
The scary thoughts of lightning striking a post,
The nights of dreams, of scary ghosts.
The yawning of a dying whale
And the never-ending jail.

Anna Powell (10)
Castle Court School, Wimborne

Emerald

The colour of a dragon's eye is this
Glinting in its cavern dark
The colour of a snake's hiss
About to eat the skylark
The colour of an emerald bird
Glimpsed in the jungle green
The colour of a Basilisk lizard
There's a mark where it's just been
The colour of other planets' skies
With the sound of aliens' cries
The colour of an alligator swimming by
Making it look so wise.

Oliver Alder (10)
Castle Court School, Wimborne

Leaves

Intense green, blossoming leaves
Young, dazzling, blossoming leaves

Huge, vivid, radiant leaves
Glossy, emerald, radiant leaves

Crumpled, auburn, falling leaves
Furrowed, graceful, falling leaves

Frosty, brittle, deceased leaves
Lifeless, bleak, deceased leaves

Intense, green, blossoming leaves
Young, dazzling, blossoming leaves.

Joe Payne (11)
Castle Court School, Wimborne

Colours Of The Country

Red is the colour of a rose blooming,
Red is the colour of autumn looming.

Orange is the colour of a fox hunting,
Orange is the colour of crops waving.

Yellow is the colour of a tulip swaying,
Yellow is the colour of buttercups dancing.

Green is the colour of a leaf falling,
Green is the colour of meadows stirring.

Blue is the colour of a river flowing,
Blue is the colour of a sky's storming.

Indigo is the colour of a pansy floating,
Indigo is the colour of foxgloves rising.

Violet is the colour of a butterfly fluttering,
Violet is the colour of the heavens breaking.

Annabel Boothright (10)
Castle Court School, Wimborne

Colours Of The Rainbow

Green is the colour of the dragon's eye
Purple is the colour of a stormy sky
Yellow is the colour of a sandy beach
Red is the colour of a juicy peach
Pink is the colour of a tulip bud
White is the colour of a cow chewing cud
Orange is the colour of the blazing sun
Blue is the colour of the uke I strum.

Will Hosford (11)
Castle Court School, Wimborne

The Weeping Willow

The weeping willow stands gracefully by the flowing river,
The dappled sunlight shining through the swaying leaves.

In the winter it looks like a miserable, ancient green mop,
Sticking out of the ground,
Cold and lost, longing for the long winter days to be over.

It is a whole world for many different insects,
A safe haven for birds
And provides a good wind shelter for anything living.

In the summer, the children come and have picnics
Under the outstretched branches,
Playing around the broad trunk.
The willow, graceful once more.

Harry Middleton (10)
Castle Court School, Wimborne

Trees

The golden leaves rustled as the
Wind whistled to the sound
Of the long, dark night
The branches gently swayed
As the rain pounded
Onto the ground
The night drifted away
Into the light

The leaves glistened as the
Blinding sun shone upon them
The branches danced to the gentle song of the wind
Each tree has their own
Special touch of life.

Edward Southgate (9)
Castle Court School, Wimborne

Trees

They stand tall, the magnificent pines
So tall and straight, proud and strong
They grow in groups, huddled together
Does it keep them warm or are they all just friends?
They gently rustle as if whispering together.

Shaven Christmas trees in hiding
Wind moving them to its own pulse
Strong trunks swaying majestically
Orange, bumpy bark, reaching high to the heavens
Sometimes silently shearing off their needles
Which land on the ground as gently as a feather

High up, at the peak, needles grow in clusters
So straight and sharp, hiding the newborn cones
Protecting them from harm, safe inside their nest
The sharp spikes grow in groups, like soft, green clouds
Shrouding their true form in mystery
They float in ever-changing patterns against the sky
Like candyfloss on a stick.

Maxwell Noble (9)
Castle Court School, Wimborne

A Tree Is A . . .

A tree is a wooden statue, that stands silently
throughout the whole year.
A tree is a dazzling work of art and culture.
A trees is a glorious sign of the beautiful countryside.
A tree is a beautiful house where people stay warm and dry.
A trees is a fountain, the water drops from its leaves.
A trees is a superb shelter that protects from the sun.
A tree is a playground that children climb and swing on.
A tree is a bench, so comfy and so smooth.

Harry Wheildon (9)
Castle Court School, Wimborne

The Football Tree

He's as wise as an owl
And as old as time;
His branches are like
A tangled up rhyme.

To be by the tree,
Where I think a lot,
Makes me feel blessed
For the good things I've got.

Year by year,
January to December,
I've known him as long
As I can remember.

Annabel Snook (9)
Castle Court School, Wimborne

Hairy Palm

Great stringy fingers
Whistling in the wind
Bristling me as I hide.
Tower of force
In a hurricane.
Symbol of summer
Silhouetted against sunsets.
Natural umbrella
Deflecting the light
Protecting me.
My favourite tree.

Arthur Bowden (10)
Castle Court School, Wimborne

Autumn Trees

We're out to play
On a nippy old day.
With autumn all around,
There are amber leaves
Looking like flame in the trees,
Or even scarlet handkerchiefs,
Fluttering in the blustery breeze.

Tiny bugs scuttle up and down the trunk,
As if racing to reach the summit.
Then the excitement on the trees comes clear;
A wren flies down, sparking fear.
Darting here, hopping there, insects scatter everywhere.
Peck! She got one; a juicy, squirming beetle.
Slurp! It's gone, sliding down her throat.

The breeze turns into a squall
And a tree begins to fall.
Golden leaves waft down
Like king's jewels dropping from gnarled fingers.
As the wind starts to bite
The roots cling on tight.

Night creeps in early in autumn,
The wind subsides and all is still.
Birds and beetles have melted into the darkness;
All that remains is the gentle rustle of leaves,
As if whispering goodnight.

Tim Rutland (9)
Castle Court School, Wimborne

Rainforest Trees

In the forest trees grow so high
Looking up they block the sky

Canopies lush that spread so far
At night no light from a single star

By day the forest is alive
And makes it easy to survive

For all God's creatures, great and small
Living in these trees so tall

The snake is looking for his chance
While baby monkeys jump and dance

Ants and spiders search their way
The trees providing all their prey

Is that a leaf before my eyes
Or a butterfly in disguise?

Brown and green and golden hue
And sap attracting mites like glue

How wondrous is this world of trees
To pray I get down on my knees

For all God's creatures, great and small
Living in these trees so tall.

Jack James Martin (9)
Castle Court School, Wimborne

Me - The Tree

Magnificent, majestic, mighty me, the tree
Breezy winds blowing through my branches
Sizzling sun penetrating my leaves
Fresh, thirst-quenching rain
Oh, what a wonderful life I lead
Magnificent, majestic, mighty me, the tree.

Irritated, irate, infuriated me, the tree
Bulky boys weighing down my branches
Inconsiderate imbeciles peeling away my bark
Disobedient dogs digging up my roots
Oh, how disgruntled I am
Irritated, irate, infuriated me, the tree

Cheerful, cheery, contented me, the tree
Heavenly hummingbirds singing enchanted songs
Amazing ant armies tickling my limbs
Girls giggling, playing and having fun
Oh, what a gleeful life I lead
Cheerful, cheery, contented me, the tree.

Harry Agombar (9)
Castle Court School, Wimborne

Trees

Trees, trees, trees,
Big ones, small ones,
Green ones in spring,
Brown ones in autumn,
Evergreen, all year long,
Blossom in the spring,
Nuts in autumn,
Trees help us to breathe,
Trees, trees, trees.

Georgina Tucker (9)
Castle Court School, Wimborne

My Apple Tree

In springtime, fat buds burst into delicate, white blossom,
Little birds make their nests in the beauty of its branches,
The blossom falls softly, like snow.

In summer, emerald leaves flutter and wave in the heat,
The feathery fledglings take their first flights
In the safety of its branches.

In autumn, rosy red apples drop heavily onto the dewy grass,
Sweet and deliciously juicy in my mouth,
Crisp and crunchy, red, orange and yellow leaves drift to the ground.

Wintertime, my tree is a skeleton,
The trunk twinkles in the freezing frost,
Still a home for the birds,
But it looks sad,
Waiting, waiting for spring . . .

Rosie Hellewell (9)
Castle Court School, Wimborne

Food

What is brown, melts in your mouth
And is bought in squares?
A chocolate block.

What is green and red, round
And grows on a tree?
An apple.

What is red,
With a green spiky hat on top?
A tomato.

What comes in straight, spirally shapes
And a bow tie?
Pasta.

Samuel Wheeler (9)
Castle Court School, Wimborne

Trees

Trees, twisting, turning trunks,
Leaves, blood-red, glowing in the sunlight like a burning torch,
You see huge trunks of the mighty oak,
You hear the rustling from the leaves overhead.

A tree bending, almost to snapping with fruit, apples, apricots ,
Mouth-wateringly juicy
Standing mighty and tall
As far as the eye can see.
A world of insects, birds, even worms
Are all part of this wooden world.

Trees blowing in the wind but holding firm,
you can feel its rough edges
trees, providing
food for us, nuts, berries, they taste delicious,
a whole larder.

A tree, looping, entangling, stretching and twisting around everything,
A tree, a beautiful tree, blazing colours, beautifully formed trunk,
Moving out in all directions,
Standing out in the sunset
Like a figure standing in the sunset.

You can see things in the tree;
People, animals, other plants, a house, anything.
A tree is a fantastic object.

Henry Imms (9)
Castle Court School, Wimborne

A Green, Slimy Cricket

I would like to touch . . .
The words of a green, slimy cricket,
The whisper of God's voice telling us what to do,
The screams of a fiery comet flying down to Earth.

I would like to hear . . .
The sun on a Christmas Day,
The magic of music,
The flowers reaching towards the sky.

I would like to understand . . .
The squeak of my guinea pigs,
The roar of a lion,
The magic of my brain.

I would like to take home the . . .
Magic of the moon and place it in a container
Hotness of the sun,
Fury of a werewolf,
Fizz of Coca-Cola.

I would like to imagine . . .
Clouds were made of candyfloss,
Wind was made of water,
Walls were made of glorious cheese.

Harrison Jones (8)
Castle Court School, Wimborne

Trees

They are tall or wide,
They are green outside.
How many are there
In the world wide?
Some are young,
Some are old,
In the heat
Or in the cold.
They have flowers and seeds,
Make a home for the bees,
Food for squirrels and birds.
They shelter the cattle,
With the wind they battle.
They give oxygen for men
And wood for a den.
They dance in the breeze,
In the winter they freeze
And lose their leaves.
But now, in the spring,
They dream of the sun.
Their new life has begun.

Toby Woodhouse (9)
Castle Court School, Wimborne

Trees

A tree can change its colour,
From bright green to red and gold,
Then shed its leaves in autumn,
As the temperature turns cold.

A tree can give us shelter,
From the burning summer sun,
As we play in our garden,
Safe, but having fun.

A tree can give protection,
From a damaging, gusty storm,
It gives us wood to heat our homes,
Keeping us so very warm

A tree can be a cosy place,
For a bird to build his nest,
And for squirrels searching nuts,
Who pause to take a rest.

A tree can give us all so much,
Like paper, in books we read,
They give great beauty to our world,
And clean air that we need.

Benjamin Battey (9)
Castle Court School, Wimborne

Food

Chicken, oh chicken, it's wonderful stuff.
Chicken, oh chicken, can't get enough.
Scrumptious and tasty with lots of lovely flavours,
Chicken, oh chicken, it brings in the neighbours.

Sitr-fry, oh stir-fry, it's a lovely thing,
Stir-fry, oh stir-fry, it makes me sing,
Stir-fry, oh stir-fry, I love it a lot,
Stir-fry, oh stir-fry, it is quite hot.

Chocolate, oh chocolate, it melts in the mouth,
Chocolate, oh chocolate, makes me go south,
Chocolate, oh chocolate, you really taste good,
Chocolate, oh chocolate, I eat you with pud.

Carrots, oh carrots, all crunchy and great,
Carrots, oh carrots, I eat you on a plate.
But now my food poem is all but done,
I just want to tell you, it was very fun!

Luke Robinson (8)
Castle Court School, Wimborne

Melon Oh, Lemon Oh

Melon, oh melon, come with me.
Melon, oh melon, you are so squashy.
Melon, oh melon, you are so lovely.

Lemon, oh lemon,
I like you as much as melon!
I like you on my pancake,
Lemon in my pie,
You are tasty.
Why not try?

Felix Scull (9)
Castle Court School, Wimborne

Yummy, Yummy, In My Tummy

Luscious lemons, crispy carrots, chocolate is the best of all.
Ice cream, spicy sausage and lovely gingerbread dwarf,
I can't get over that syrupy tart and spicy pizzas to eat
And lots and lots of sweets.

Cola, cola, fantastic Fanta, cheesy crisps are nice to taste,
But wobbly jelly is nice in your belly,
Chewy cherry, a fantastic berry.

Indigestible ice cream, creamy cake, toxic tomatoes,
Mouth-watering melon, super strawberries, chocolate-coated caramel,
It's super duper, swell,
Candy canes spread all around,
Happiness is always found.

Rupert Peter Ward Bennett (9)
Castle Court School, Wimborne

Sprouts, Sprouts, Sprouts

Sprouts are like crunchy, burnt jamón
They smell like gone off salmon
It's not very cool
It's round as a ball.

Sprouts are round as a mud bomb
Sprouts are squidgy as a pom-pom ball
They're green, like cabbage
Eat too much and they'll cause you damage.

Oliver Jessup (8)
Castle Court School, Wimborne

The Incredible Trees

Breathtaking trees twist and turn
Ruby-red leaves swoosh and whoosh in the brisk wind
Redwood, Douglas fir, Spruce
The tallest in the world
Spiky bark
Smooth bark
Silky leaves slip from your hands
Glittering frost sets so beautifully on the leaves
The glorious colours of the leaves blaze out from the trunk
The hole for the woodpecker
The branches to make nests for the birds
To keep the animals safe
From predators
The proud trees stand so strong, forever long.

Georgina Carter (9)
Castle Court School, Wimborne

Fabulous Me

I am one thousand per cent fabulous.
People die looking at my beautiful face
And everyone loves my voice.
I'm the kindest and the best in the world.
My teacher has a shock when I do my maths test.
I'm the main part of the pantomime,
I never show off!

Fabulous,
Fabulous
Me!

Alexandra Sanders (8)
Castle Court School, Wimborne

Yummy In My Tummy

Crunchy chocolate, crispy, sweet,
Cakes and ice cream, can't be beat,
Jelly is a luscious treat,
With lots and lots of pie to eat.

Sizzling, delicious, glorious
Pizza party, luxurious,
Chocolate-coated caramel,
It is super-duper, swell.

Lots and lots of fizzy pop,
Would make you sit and drink a drop,
Yummy, juicy orange squash,
Would be worth a load of dosh.

Tasty, squashy marshmallows,
Makes you smile from head to toe,
Yorkshire pudding, piled high,
Reaching up to the sky.

Tommy Bridger (8)
Castle Court School, Wimborne

Food

Chocolate, chocolate, you're so good!
Chocolate, chocolate, great for pud!

Grapefruit, grapefruit, you're not yummy,
Grapefruit, grapefruit, keep out of my tummy.

Ice cream, ice cream,
I scream for ice cream.

I will set you a little test,
Sprout or bogie, which is best?

Henry Baugniet (9)
Castle Court School, Wimborne

Food Poem

Food, food, a ring-a-ding-ding,
Food, food, you make me sing.
Fizzy Fanta, Diet Coke,
Passion fruit is fashion fruit.

Lemons and limes and apples too,
Sweet and sour, the taste in my mouth,
Meat, meat, I'll eat you up.

Meat, meat, you're so great,
Sugar sweet,
Crisps and chips,
Coke and Fanta you are so yummy,
You start to mix in my tummy.

Deserts are my favourite,
Ice cream,
In many flavours,
None are yucky,
Caramel chocolate is so very mucky.

Food, food, towering jelly,
Yum-yum, in my belly.

William Jacobs (8)
Castle Court School, Wimborne

Chocolate

Chocolate, chocolate, you are so great,
I'd love to be your best mate.
Chocolate, chocolate, you sell very well,
I love to buy you when you sell.

Chocolate, chocolate, you taste so great,
You are lovely on a cake.
I love you on pancakes,
I love chocolate chips
Because they taste so great.

Luciano De Bacci (8)
Castle Court School, Wimborne

Wobbly Jelly

Jelly, jelly, wobbles like mad,
Everyone is so sad,
When it's gone.
Jelly, you are not so bad!

You can't get enough of it,
Even if you try,
Just have a taste and see what you think!
Jelly, jelly, wobbles in my tummy.

Shines like a ruby in the light,
I love it when I see you on my plate,
I have stacks of it in my fridge,
I have it for pudding every day!

But it's even better with ice cream,
It's great and tasty,
It's delicious,
So tasty it makes you want to scream!

Alfred Streeton (9)
Castle Court School, Wimborne

Fantastic Food

Chocolate, chocolate, fudge as well,
These are the things I like to smell.
Caramel and toffee are tasty things,
Sweets just always make me sing.

Jelly, jelly, oh, wonderful stuff,
This is squelchy, I can't get enough.
Jelly, jelly, so tasty and luscious,
Jelly, jelly, I love you muchas!

Alastair Carter (9)
Castle Court School, Wimborne

Salad And Cheddar Cheese

Salad, oh salad, I hate you so much
You look like a piece of mint
You are so smelly you make me feel sick to my tummy
You taste quite funny
Salad, salad, you are disgusting
All squished up.

Cheddar cheese on my plate
Cheddar cheese, Cheddar cheese
I love you so much
You are so yummy, I want you so
You are so scrummy in my tummy.

Edward Southgate (8)
Castle Court School, Wimborne

Food Poem

Jelly, jelly, it wobbles in my belly,
Garlic is so very smelly.
Golden treacle is very scrummy,
It melts in my tummy.

Pickled shallots, there are lots,
Even when they're in pots,
They've got spice
Which makes them nice.

Rice is so lovely
And nice,
So is
Egg fried rice.

Kyle Flower (9)
Castle Court School, Wimborne

Ten Things Found In A Witch's Pocket

A big wart cut in half.
Some babies who are holding some scissors.
A big frog who is sick.
Some people who shrink.
A little snail who is sticking to her.
Some water.
A large mouse.
A big blue wand.
A little yellow broomstick.
Some of her fingers.

Rosie Southgate (7)
Castle Court School, Wimborne

Me, Me, Me

I am one hundred per cent fabulous,
I am the most popular,
Everyone laughs at my jokes,
Everyone thinks I am funny,
Everyone who knows me
Knows that I am the best,
Nobody can beat me in a running race,
I'm better than a champion
At everything there is,
I'm better than my teacher,
I'm amazingly intelligent,
All my family love me,
They know that I'm the best,
My friends and cousins love me,
It's all about me, me, me!

Lucy Chapple (8)
Castle Court School, Wimborne

I Rule The World

I'm the artist of the world,
When Miss Milnes sees my maths she faints with amazement.
I'm the best . . . best . . . at hockey,
I always score the goals!

I always have a gold sticker.
Mr Nicholl gets his flags out when he sees me!
I've passed all my exams.
I can play 'Smoke on the Water' on my guitar,
I play for Razorlight.

I qualify for the England rugby team,
The coach told me.
My mum loves me the most
And I love beans on toast.

I rule the world!

Chris Rutland (8)
Castle Court School, Wimborne

A Butterfly Poem

When the butterflies come out
The flowers start to sprout
And the birds sing merrily
The bees begin to buzz
And the children play happily
All underneath the church.

Nicola Nuttall (8)
Castle Court School, Wimborne

I'd Like To . . .

I would like to paint . . .
The sound of the cricket,
My heart filled with joy,
The sparkle of the tooth fairy.

I would like to touch . . .
The sun so hot,
The shimmery reflection of a blossoming tree,
The top of the tallest tree.

I would like to jump . . .
Down to the deepest oceans
In a big ship's wake,
Into the worlds above.

Tom Tombs (9)
Castle Court School, Wimborne

I Would Like To . . .

I would like to paint . . .
The heart that thumps like a drum,
The sweet scent of blossom,
All the colours of the wind.

I would like to feel . . .
The magic pot of gold running down the rainbow,
All the voices of the mountains,
Dark wolves howling at the moon.

I would like to imagine . . .
A giant tree touching Heaven,
The night that is still,
Candyfloss in the sky.

Megan Griffiths (9)
Castle Court School, Wimborne

I Would Like To Paint

I would like to paint . . .
The noise of thunder
The beat of my heart
The beautiful noise of a zebra when it neighs
The coldness of snowflakes
The hotness of the sun
The fireworks going bang every now and again.

I should take home . . .
The future and put it in a box
The hotness and the coldness of winter
The rainbow to colour my room
The crackle of a fire
The sound of hyenas laughing
The noise of my dog.

I would like to touch . . .
Heaven, while I'm still alive
The lightning shocking at the speed of light
The core of the Earth
The Roman gods.

I would like to understand . . .
The speaking of a dog
The hiss of a snake
The roar of a lion.

I would like to surf on . . .
The clouds
A giant oak.

I would like to be . . .
Pluto
But best of all,
I'd like to be who I am.

Thomas Powell (9)
Castle Court School, Wimborne

I Would Like To Paint . . .

I would like to paint . . .
The breeze on a windy day,
The roar of a hungry lion,
The heart of Jupiter's red spot.

I would like to touch . . .
The happiness of a newborn baby,
The beautiful colours of the rainbow,
The sun rising on a summer's day.

I would like to take home . . .
A huge elephant,
A small, fluffy cat,
A roaring tiger.

I would like to understand . . .
How birds fly,
How spiders grow their legs,
How deep the sea is.

I would like to fly . . .
Around in space,
To the tops of the trees,
Around the globe.

I would like to swim,
Through candyfloss,
Through the sky,
To the core of the Earth.

Oliver Groat (8)
Castle Court School, Wimborne

I Would Like To . . .

I would like to paint the blustery wind,
Happiness when happy,
Or even paint the echo of a clock at midnight,
The sound of crunching leaves.

I should like to handle the boiling hot sun,
Or touch the reflection on the water on a summer's day.
I would like to hear Santa's reindeer on my roof,
Or hear a beautiful flower growing.

I would like to think there is a big tree round the world,
Or imagine that Pluto is a giant daddy planet.
I would like to believe that there is a sweet land somewhere,
I would like to understand how God made me.

I would like to take home a shining star,
Or the very oldest pyramids.
I would like to soar through the fluffy clouds,
Or through the bottomless ocean.

I would like to wade through the icing on a cake,
Or sail to the sun,
Glide through fluffy clouds,
Or even surf through a computer.

Rosie Alder (9)
Castle Court School, Wimborne

Something Weird

I would like to hear . . .
The Earth spinning.
A bird swooping.
The Titanic rocking.

I would like to touch . . .
Pluto, from Earth.
The burning hot core of the Earth.
The freezing cold of Pluto.

I would like to imagine . . .
Clouds were candyfloss.
I was an asteroid heading for the sun.

I would like to take home . . .
Mercury
To sunbathe in the sun's heat.

I would like to understand . . .
Why space is so big.
Why Saturn is the 6th planet from the sun.
Why butterflies fly.

Harrison Faull (8)
Castle Court School, Wimborne

I Would Like To Paint . . .

I would like to paint . . .
The wind whistling and whirling,
The sound of crackling and burning of fire,
Lightning coming down from the sky.

I would like to hear . . .
The heartbeat of a mute swan,
The moon revolving the Earth,
A comet melting.

I would like to imagine . . .
Surfing on candyfloss clouds,
Playing rugby on Pluto,
Flying through giant trees.

I would like to take home . . .
A tiny monster with one eye and three legs,
A light bag of wind,
A car powered by gases from other planets.

I would like to understand . . .
Why I can't see the top of my head
And how snakes have venom.

Leo Pembroke (8)
Castle Court School, Wimborne

I Would Like To . . .

I would like to hear . . .
Magic of the mist,
Fluffy clouds,
The scent of flowers.

I would like to touch . . .
The gold of the ground,
Heaven's roof,
The Roman gods.

I would like to imagine . . .
That space is below us,
That I am the human race,
My life never finished.

I would like to understand . . .
Animals talking,
Why I was made
And who made me.

I would like to fly . . .
Through the deep sea,
Surf through the clouds,
To the sun and back.

Maia Knowles (8)
Castle Court School, Wimborne

How I Would Like To . . .

Touch my heart on Father's Day.
Paint a lion when it wakes on a morning day.
Stroke the beautiful smell of my mother's perfume.
Imagine the clouds were made of candyfloss.
Smell the scent of the sun.
Touch God.
Hear candyfloss.
Touch the Devil.
Sail to the world's end.
Draw the Milky Way.
Sketch a frog on a lily pad.
I would like to pat Pluto.
I would like to soar through electricity.

Henry Halewood (9)
Castle Court School, Wimborne

Food

Cherry fool, you are so great,
I love to see you on my plate.
Cake, oh cake, I love to bake,
Also milkshakes are nice to shake.

Cake, cake, you're a good thing,
I love to eat you from a tin.
Sprouts, sprouts, you're so gross,
I hate to eat you with my roast.
Hot dogs, hot dogs, you're so good,
But I do not like you with my pud.

Broccoli, broccoli, it's not wrong,
Mum says it will make me big and strong.
Rum, rum, you're so yum,
I love to feel you in my tum.

Arthur Cordwell (8)
Castle Court School, Wimborne

Brown Is Not Boring

Brown is the colour of a crackled autumn leaf, gliding to the ground.
Brown is the colour of a tall, old tree.
Brown is the colour of my boxer dog.
Brown is the colour of a chestnut horse.
Brown is the colour of my rugby shirt.
Brown is the colour of very burnt toast.
Brown is the colour of an off banana.
Brown is the colour of a country pancake.
Brown is the colour of a dead, wet tree.
Brown is the colour of rotting beef.
Brown is the colour of my muddy welly boots.
Brown is the colour of Biba's fur.
Brown is the colour of my chocolate cat's fur.
Brown is the colour of my eyes and my hair.
Brown is everywhere!

Oliver Jones (10)
Castle Court School, Wimborne

Colours

Lime is the colour of juicy, refreshing fruit.
Green's the colour of a tree about to bloom.
White is a mercy flag held high.
Scarlet is the colour of blood from a bleeding wound.
Sapphire is the colour of a sapphire, dazzling in the sun.
Grey is the colour of the sky on a gloomy morning.
Blue is the colour of the sky and seas.

Alex Waller-Edwards (11)
Castle Court School, Wimborne

Lime

Lime is the colour of some people's eyes.
Lime is as cool as lemonade,
Green with silver threads of gold.
Citrus, sparkly, juicy and plump.
Streaks of lemon and lime,
Sharp and sweet at the same time.
Spring lime, jumping into summer,
Diving into lime-green jelly.
Lime marmalade on hot, buttery toast.
Plump, lime sweets in big glass jars in the sweet shop.
Lime is the colour of a new spring day.
Lime is sharp when it tingles down your throat.
Lime sherbets, fizzing and tangy.
Sunlight catching lime leaves through the trees makes me happy.

Thomas Erbetta (10)
Castle Court School, Wimborne

Colours

Blue is the colour of a summer sky
Black is a bird flying up high
Yellow is the sun so bright
White is the twinkling stars at night
Orange is my favourite sweet
Peach is the colour of my size three feet
Green is the smell of freshly cut grass
Silver is the coating on a frosted glass
Copper is the pipe that brings water to drink
Gold is my mum's bracelet link
Brown is a Galaxy chocolate bar
Pink is a silly colour for a car
Rainbow is a child's beach ball
And red is my favourite colour of all!

Giovanni De Bacci (10)
Castle Court School, Wimborne

Colours

Of swirling grey mists and blue, frosty mountains,
Of purple storms and the strong, mauve wind,
Of navy blue seas and black depressing clouds,
Of white, glittering snow and shining, silver frost.

Of fresh lime mornings and dense jade clovers,
Of growing mint leaves and dead, yellow grass,
Of peppermint flowers and ripe, green gooseberries,
Of long lemon ferns waving in the spring breeze.

Of lilac summer evenings and lazy orange lunches,
Of Moroccan days at the beach and red days in the garden,
Of clear blue skies and white fluffy clouds,
Of a Tuscan sea breeze and the saffron sands in the Sahara.

Of blazing orange campfires and a golden leaf blanket,
Of ginger-coloured hazelnuts and sleeping chestnut trees,
Of burying my friends in the umber leaves,
Of drinking milk and honey when I was feeling blue.

Bryony Bennett (11)
Castle Court School, Wimborne

Colours

Red is the colour of love.
Purple is the best colour sweet of Quality Street.
Black is the colour that sucks you into a deep, dark hole.
Blue is the colour of a deep, deep sleep.
Green is full of envy and evil.
Orange is the blazing of a burning fire.

Daisy Poole (11)
Castle Court School, Wimborne

The Trees That Woke By Night

The tree, reaches out with its branches, like claws
And the hole in its trunk looks like wide open jaws.
The winding, twisting and confusing roots
Resemble a pair of rotting, old boots.

And in the night the winding willow likes to weep,
Whilst the owl twitters and hoots as you try hard to sleep.
And in the still of the night, the leaves start to sway,
Ready to fall on the ground on a crisp and cold day.

And like a tiny insect on a broken twig,
In the darkness, I am so small next to the oak, so big.
As I shout loudly, playing my favourite game
Deep in the forest the trees echo my name.

If you can tell a tree's age by their number of rings
I'm sure if they could talk, they'd tell you many things . . .

Tamar Tucker-Harrison (10)
Castle Court School, Wimborne

Tree Poem

Trees are all different shapes and sizes
Some big and some small
They look like old grannies
So I watch them sway and the leaves fall

The leaves are brown, yellow and orange
They are coloured like parchment
When you step on them they go crackle and crunch
It smells earthy and rusty.

Louisa De Paola (10)
Castle Court School, Wimborne

The Tree

On a bitter winter's night, the tree stands alone
Towering over me and the ground far below
Like a hunchback giant
Dark and menacing against the faint moonlight

Twisted limbs reach for me
Needle fingers grasp and snag my clothes
Damp, scaly skin grates against my cheek
And a jagged, uneven mouth holds a sinister smile

I struggle to escape
As twig fingers snap in the quiet of the night
And gnarled roots wrap around my desperate feet
I fall into a smothering cloak of darkness

Running away through the fields
I glance back at the tree
Planted like a statue for countless more winters
So lonely and sad, it calls me back.

Oscar Brooks (9)
Castle Court School, Wimborne

Trees

The menacing power of trees
With roots as thick as chimneys
The trunk as wide as a double gate
As tall as the Empire State
It is the nightmare you fear every night

The scariest thing you have ever seen
It will crush you to a tiny bean
You see a small tree, nice and friendly
But dark shadows tower - it's not so heavenly
Long branches of menacing power suffocate

So never go into a forest in the dead of night
It might give you a terrible fright.

Alex Schuster-Bruce (10)
Castle Court School, Wimborne

Trees

I wonder if trees could grow under the seas
Just like they do on the land.
Would the branches grow high, to some distant sky?
Would their roots dig deep in the sand?
Would the little fish play
In their branches by day?
Sharks and whales seek the roots
Of that forest so deep
And while storms rage and blow
In the deep, down below,
All that seaweedy forest's asleep.

Do you think trees could grow under the seas
Just like they do on the land?
With leafy fronds waving, the crest of waves breaking,
Their treetops on view to the strand?
The turtles would plant them,
Sea witches enchant them,
To hide sleeping beauties away.
Cold currents would blow them,
Sea horses would know them,
They'd hide little mermaids by day.

I'm sure there are trees growing under the seas,
Just like they do on the land.
For I've heard of a branch that was washed up by chance
On the shores of a far distant land.
The sea there is deep
And when I'm asleep,
I dream of that forest so rare,
Where sea creatures graze
And Mer-people laze,
Come join me to find them - I'll dare!

George Acworth (10)
Castle Court School, Wimborne

Tree Journey

I see it in silhouette on the rugged hillside, black, sharp fingers
stretching skywards.
I run excitedly, sweating, eager to climb, ready for the challenge.
As I near, I see a mighty oak, mature, old and majestic,
demanding my respect.
Its bark is gnarled, wrinkled and weathered from the battering winds
on the hill.
I seize my opportunity, a huge branch beckoning me on.
My fingers grip tightly and I heave myself upwards, branch by branch,
securing my balance like my life depends on it.
An earthy smell hits my senses and the bark feels slippy
from the evening dew.
I startle a squirrel and it scurries away like a cheetah running
for its prey.
I wobble and grab at a piece of bark, a loud crack and it splinters,
falling like an arrow on the strike.
An army of termites, brown with large heads and fierce jaws, squirm
and ooze and I jump backwards with alarm.
I catch my footing, grit my teeth and continue on, eager to reach
the top, knowing that I'm fighting against the mighty, twisted strength
of the tree and all its secrets.
Soft, velvety leaves rub against my skin, it soothes my fear
and I hear a woodpigeon cooing its twilight song.
As I near the top of the tree happiness overcomes me
and an amazing view of neatly patchworked English countryside
stretches out before me.
I feel free!

Alistair Warr (9)
Castle Court School, Wimborne

The World Of A Tree

Standing tall and proud,
Always watching over you.
From the sky scraping of an oak
To the weeping of the willow.
Their spring buds burst beautifully like butterflies from a chrysalis,
Their winter branches point, like wrinkly fingers,
at things you cannot reach.
Their autumn leaves, coloured like flames,
that twist and twirl toward the ground.
Summer sunlight casts wonderful shadows through the dense
canopies.
Strong roots, tied to the earth,
Go in search of nourishment.
The tree protects and shelters us when we need,
from wind, rain and snow.
Our thanks to God for these knowing creatures,
Earth's source of life.

Sebastian Fletcher (9)
Castle Court School, Wimborne

The Tree

Spring is here, the
tree awakes.
Buds abound waiting
to bloom.
Branches outstretched
to reach the sky.
The leaves explode and
show their magnificence
creating shade in the hot
summer sun.
Autumn arrives and
with it comes glorious colour
red, yellow, orange and brown.
Down fall these leaves
majestic no more
the tree stands alone
skeletal and poor.

Alexander Stocks (9)
Castle Court School, Wimborne

The Tree At The Back Of My Garden

The tree over there, yes, that's it, isn't really a tree at all
In fact I think it even talks.
It sits there and stares at me,
As if it can really walk and talk.
But these stupid tales, of wind whistling through trees,
Of bees silently buzzing past the autumn leaves
And of old fir trees on Christmas Eve,
I really think these are not for me.
But since I saw the tall willow tree,
I saw what they are all about.
They are for being with, for looking at,
Yes, so that's what they're for.
They're not only for us though,
But for the beautiful singing birds
And as the leaves drop down
They make a wonderful crunchy sound.
For the birds rustling in the trees
Is just the chicks hatching with ease.
The tree may look very old
But he still lives in this world
And so does the world within him.

Harry Schotel (10)
Castle Court School, Wimborne

My Walk Through The Woods

As I walk through the forest
I hear the crunch of leaves
And the waving of the branches
And the rustle of the trees.

Tall trees and small trees
Majestically looking down at me
Like a colourful and vibrant circus
What an interesting sight to see.

Suddenly, I hear a noise
What could it be?
Is it a fox or even a wolf . . . ?
Oh, it's only a starling in a tree!

I can feel the wind in my hair
Like a lion, roaring in my face
Raindrops start to fall
So I quicken up my pace.

So pleased am I to be home
All cosy and warm
So I snuggle up on the sofa
And dream about all I saw!

Ella Clayton (9)
Castle Court School, Wimborne

Colours

Blue is the colour of the sky,
Blue is the colour of my eye,
Blue is the colour of the sea,
Blue is the colour of my key.

Yellow is the colour of my shirt,
Yellow is the colour of my skirt,
Yellow is the colour of the sand,
Yellow is the colour of the sun.

Red is the colour of love,
Red is the colour of blood,
Red is the colour of a dragon's eye,
Red is the colour of an evil sigh.

Green is the colour of a weed,
Green is the colour of my dog's lead,
Green is the colour of leaves,
Green is the colour of kiwis.

Victoria Webb (9)
Castle Court School, Wimborne

Blue

Blue is the colour of a clear blue sky
Cloudless, cold and bright
Blue is the tear that falls from my eye
When I remember old memories
Blue is the colour of the deep blue sea
All the fishes glistening
Blue are the eyes that help me see
How could I do without them?
Blue is the mood when I'm unhappy
And I'm sighing with sadness
Blue is the bird's wing in the glimmering tree
Flapping in the sun
Blue is the colour of my favourite shirt
New, clean and dry
Blue is my ball, lost in dirt
Flat from the thorns and bushes
Blue are my jeans, scuffed at the knee
Just as I've been playing
Blue is a wonderful colour to me.

James Mullins (11)
Castle Court School, Wimborne

Our Autumn Wood

(In the autumn, Badger Class spent an afternoon exploring the woods near the school. Each pupil wrote a descriptive couplet and, as a class, we put them all together)

Near school is a wood
A woody wood
A colourful, secret, woody wood
So we went to explore

We walked, no talking
We heard leaves and twigs
We heard crunchy leaves and snappy twigs
And rain hitting the leaves
High up in the trees

On rotten trunks we saw pink toadstools
Huge brown toadstools
Massive eaten toadstools
And tiny ones, like new potatoes

In secret places
We found slugs
We found tiny slugs, black beetles, silver woodlice
And a black, furry spider's cave

We sat and watched the leaves
Caterpillar-green leaves
Ruby and chocolate leaves
Lava-orange, noodle-yellow and golden syrup leaves
Luscious lemon and lime drizzle leaves!
All falling silently

We discovered
Mole hills
Sandy mole hills with holes
Deer tracks and a badger sett
The secret life of the wood

The wood was full of smells
Strong smells
Earth and bark smells
Garlic, ginger and muddy smells
Like Wookey Hole Caves!
We felt excited and happy
Touching bark and soft moss
Finding a dinosaur of rotten wood
We loved getting wet and soggy
In our beautiful autumn wood.

Badger Class
Chewton Mendip CE (VA) School, Chewton Mendip

Frost

Gliding on the shining leaves,
I see, I see Jack Frost
Waking and making the animals jump.
Leaving all his icicle diamonds behind
I see, I see, I see crystal-white
There is frost on my car
That is his trail
I see tiny lights of teardrops
I see something blue
Gliding on the silver frost
I see, I see, I see
Jack Frost!

Tayla Carlsson (9)
Corpus Christi Catholic Primary School, Boscombe

Frost

Jack Frost, Jack Frost,
Swooping down to Earth
As graceful as a dove,
Leaving pearly white teardrops.

Jack Frost, Jack Frost,
Lustrous white gems of beauty,
He leaves in a dusty, sparkling trail.

Jack Frost, Jack Frost,
His deadly icicles, which have no mercy,
Bite into leaves, into trees!

Jack Frost, Jack Frost,
Drifts away, never to be seen again,
Morphs into water,
One final admiration of his long and tiring work,
Vanishes, teleports . . .
Hides away . . .

Until the next great Ice Age.

Connor Rowlett (9)
Corpus Christi Catholic Primary School, Boscombe

Frost

Frost comes in wintertime,
Covering the ground
Like silky, white snow.

Frost makes your fingers cold
When you touch it,
Like when you touch snow.

Aleasha Mallon (9)
Corpus Christi Catholic Primary School, Boscombe

Mr Frost

In the middle of the night,
a prowler sneaks from tree to tree, car to car,
ducking in and out of the moonlight.
He is never seen, but his presence is eerily felt.
He leaves a blanket of crystal clear ice - *Havoc!*
Diamond icicles hang stiffly from the branches and the windowpanes.
The people awake to a winter ice land.
Slippery pavements, frozen windscreens, cold breath!
But then . . .
The sun rises from his dreary den -
The world warms.
Jack Frost disappears, at least until tonight . . .

Kara Abbott (10)
Corpus Christi Catholic Primary School, Boscombe

Frost

Frost is a misty man,
That makes you want to shiver.
It doesn't seem like he's really there,
He's just a little glimmer.

Frost is a horrible man,
Who nobody really likes.
He always sneaks up on you
And gives you a terrible fright!

Frost is a nasty man,
He only visits in the night.
He leaves a trail of shimmering ice,
Don't be fooled by the lustrous sight!

Mary Roughley (9)
Corpus Christi Catholic Primary School, Boscombe

Dear Tooth Fairy

Dear Tooth Fairy,
Do you have feathery, silky wings like an angel?
Do you have soft, golden, flowing hair?
Is your skin milky white, like the teeth you collect?
What colour dress do you wear, glittering in the moonlight?
Do you have a palace made out of teeth?
Would you fly me out of my window and into the dark, starry sky?
I dream about you every day and wish you would take me to your
                                       magical fairyland far, far away.

Leila Dixon (9)
Corpus Christi Catholic Primary School, Boscombe

Autumn

The autumn wind blows the trees,
It's like snowing but with leaves.
All falling down in a range of different colours;
Red, yellow and green,
Because spring and summer have already been.

Nadine Barber (10)
Corpus Christi Catholic Primary School, Boscombe

Jack Frost

Frost, frost so very bright,
Glimmering in the dark.
Gliding through the air
Like butterflies in summertime.

Frost, frost so very light,
Lighter than a leaf falling
From a tree
At the dawn of autumn.

Frost, frost, so very *white!*

Jack Figg (9)
Corpus Christi Catholic Primary School, Boscombe

Jack Frost

The glimmering, webbed feet.
Crush through the snowy sun.
Whilst the children of the night awake
And the diamonds of winter shine through the icy waters.
As the reindeers fly through the sky of the winter night,
The icicles, of his hair, shine through the snowy mountains.
As his glittery eyes glare into the snowy surface
And the gleaming sun falls to sunset.

Daniel Hawkins (10)
Corpus Christi Catholic Primary School, Boscombe

Frost

He webs his glittery hands
Spreads his diamonds
In a meandering trail.
He glides and slips upon the ground,
Swoops back up like a . . .
Ghost!

Gaby Smith (9)
Corpus Christi Catholic Primary School, Boscombe

Frost

Jack Frost, Jack Frost,
Leaping through the falling snowflakes.
Jack Frost, Jack Frost,
Slipping swiftly past the frosty trees.
Jack Frost, Jack Frost,
Sprinkles all the teardrops.
Jack Frost, Jack Frost,
Moving swiftly through the air.
Jack Frost, Jack Frost.

Jamie Wilkinson (9)
Corpus Christi Catholic Primary School, Boscombe

Frost

Jack Frost lives in the ice, waiting for us to cross.
Jack Frost makes us freeze without any sunshine.
Jack Frost puts the glistening ice on the Earth.
Jack Frost comes to sprinkle us with stone-cold snowflakes.

As he flows from outer space, he comes in peace,
He leaves a white, glittery blanket on which we slip,
He can't live with sunshine as he will melt,
He runs away from summer.

Jack Frost lives in the ice, waiting for us to cross.
Jack Frost makes us freeze without any sunshine.
Jack Frost puts the glistening ice on the Earth.
Jack Frost comes to sprinkle us with stone-cold snowflakes.

Connor Trussell (9)
Corpus Christi Catholic Primary School, Boscombe

Frost

There's a cold, sparking man,
Who lives in an ice winter wonderland.
He comes out at night, children wake,
Animals watch, the moon hides.
But when the sun rises, oh no, he jumps away
And the world awakes.
He has left a blanket of sparkling frost
And glossy patches of diamonds are everywhere.
Lustrous fun everywhere.

Who is it?
Jack Frost.

Nicole Livesey (9)
Corpus Christi Catholic Primary School, Boscombe

Hate

Hate is blood-red, like a dragon breathing fire and snarling at you.
Hate sounds like the screaming of a burning city
and people screaming curses at their attackers.
Hate looks like the pain and suffering of a thousand different people.
Hate reminds me of guns firing little shells of death
and blood soaking the ground.
Hate feels like a towering inferno, building up inside me.
Hate tastes like blood and pain,
raging up from your heart to your throat
and then to your mouth and tongue.
Hate smells like a sickening stench of blood, pain and problems.

Samuel Maddix (10)
Court De Wyck Primary School, Claverham

Fun

Fun is black like me at the skate ramps.
It tastes like chocolate in the air.
Fun is blue like the bright sky.
It smells like fresh air, floating around us.
Fun is red like people playing in the park.
It reminds me of me and my dad playing together.
Fun is pink like my sister playing with her toys,
It looks like her laughing with her friends.
Fun feels like two people together.
Fun sounds like people alive and feeling happy.

Jack Drake (11)
Court De Wyck Primary School, Claverham

Light

Light is yellow like the sun shining through my window
on a hot summer's day.
It tastes like a piece of liquorice bought fresh from the candy shop.
It smells like a blossoming rose from my nan's garden.
It looks like the glistening blue sea.
It feels like a silky ribbon wrapped around my finger.
It sounds like the waves going up and down.
It reminds me of my mummy hugging me.

Lizzy Maddix (9)
Court De Wyck Primary School, Claverham

Sadness

Sadness is grey like a dark cloud when it's raining.
Sadness sounds like somebody crying.
Sadness, it looks like rain.
Sadness, it tastes like saltwater, (tears).
Sadness, it smells like the sea.
Sadness, it feels like rain.
Sadness reminds me of when I quit my old school.

Martin Segers (10)
Court De Wyck Primary School, Claverham

Anger

Anger is like a flickering, flaming fire.
Anger tastes like burning hot lava.
Anger smells like black smoke.
Anger looks like evil eyes at night.
Anger feels like someone ripping your heart out.
Anger sounds like someone screaming.
Anger reminds me of red-hot chillies.

Harvey Pearson (9)
Court De Wyck Primary School, Claverham

Fear

Fear is grey, like a stone in the river
Fear tastes like cold yellow cheese
Fear smells like cold air at night
Fear looks like a shadow moving about
Fear feels like a rough brown piece of wood
Fear sounds like a scream far away
Fear reminds me of me in the dark.

Elisabeth Hunt (10)
Court De Wyck Primary School, Claverham

Fun

Fun is blue like the ocean
Fun tastes like rabbit and deer
Fun smells like trial bikes' fumes
Fun looks brown like the dirt on the track
Fun feels like smooth bikes in a bike shop
Fun sounds like motocross bikes
Fun reminds me of me on my trail bike.

Zack Tinkling (11)
Court De Wyck Primary School, Claverham

Laughter

Laughter is blue like the morning sky
Laughter tastes like bluebells
Laughter smells like the fresh breeze
Laughter looks like people having fun by the sea
Laughter feels like the wind blowing on you
Laughter sounds like the Earth rumbling with happiness
Laughter reminds me of my best friend.

Chelsea Heal (9)
Court De Wyck Primary School, Claverham

Laughter

Laughter is yellow like the bright, shiny sun
Laughter tastes like a cupcake with a cherry on top
Laughter smells like the air in the summer
Laughter looks like people giggling all the time
Laughter sounds like having lots of fun
Laughter reminds me of my friends.

Sophie Cepek (9)
Court De Wyck Primary School, Claverham

Love

Love is pink like shiny, glittery hearts,
Love tastes like strawberries with sugar,
Love smells like pink and red roses,
Love looks like flickering flames,
Love feels like cuddly, soft teddy bears,
Love sounds like romantic music floating in the air,
Love reminds us of each other.

Holly Hancock (10)
Court De Wyck Primary School, Claverham

Anger

Anger is like an erupting volcano.
Anger tastes like hot chilli pepper.
Anger smells like sour sweets.
Anger reminds me of someone upsetting me.
Anger looks like a raging bull.
Anger feels like a bumpy road.
Anger sounds like a roaring dragon.

Lewis Drake (9)
Court De Wyck Primary School, Claverham

Love

Love is red like the love in my heart
Love is like you, eating chocolate
Love tastes like chocolate
Love smells like a bunch of roses
Love looks like a girl and boy kissing
Love feels like everything is tingling
Love sounds like your heart's beating
Love reminds me of my mum and dad.

Andrew Gray (10)
Court De Wyck Primary School, Claverham

Fear

Fear is black like the starry night sky
Fear looks like worried faces, like being threatened
Fear sounds like screaming voices, high-pitched in sound
Fear reminds me of people scared to death, in terror
Fear feels like being touched, with no explainable answer
Fear smells like a burning that's choking you
Fear tastes like bitter foods, sour and strong.

Lauren Victoria Blewett (10)
Court De Wyck Primary School, Claverham

Darkness

Darkness is black like evil at night
Darkness tastes like nasty liquorice in my mouth
Darkness reminds me of a thick, black cloak
Darkness looks like hot chilli
Darkness feels like an ember from a fire
Darkness sounds like cold air blowing at night
Darkness smells like vampire blood.

Daniel Summers Singleton (9)
Court De Wyck Primary School, Claverham

Silence

Silence is white like the frost on the end of your toes.
Silence tastes like a quiet room of peaceful music.
Silence smells like a quiet room with soft pillows to sleep on.
Silence looks like a quiet room with no noise at all.
Silence feels like the quietest room you can ever imagine.
Silence sounds like nothing in the room, only you.
Silence reminds me of a peaceful room with music.

Maisie E Workman (9)
Court De Wyck Primary School, Claverham

Hunger

Hunger is brown like milky, creamy chocolate.
Hunger tastes like rotten fish eggs.
Hunger smells like a hot, greasy burger.
Hunger looks like a creamy, big ice cream.
Hunger feels like a melting ice cream.
Hunger sounds like the tune on an ice cream truck.
Hunger reminds me of a double chocolate fudge cake.

Bailey Thomas (10)
Court De Wyck Primary School, Claverham

Anger

Anger is red like a sizzling fire.
Anger is hot like boiling hot soup.
Anger is hot like a spicy chilli.
Anger is smoky like a burning bonfire.
Anger is burning like a roaring fire.
Anger is boiling like a freshly baked cake.
Anger is crackling like a hot open fire.
Anger is my home fire, like a fire on a cold winter's day.

India McKeown (9)
Court De Wyck Primary School, Claverham

Hunger

Hunger is brown like bread being crushed by hands.
Hunger is like eating cheese on bread.
Hunger tastes like mouth-watering bread.
Hunger smells like flour, fresh from the field.
Hunger feels like hard bread.
Hunger sounds like a mouth chewing on food.
Hunger reminds me of a cheese burger being in my mouth.

Shane Bellotti (11)
Court De Wyck Primary School, Claverham

Love

Love is red like your heart beating.
Love smells like the scent of a red rose.
Love tastes like chocolate melting on your tongue.
Love reminds me of my baby sister when I kiss her.
Love sounds like birds singing in the moonlight.
Love feels like being in a warm bed.

Amberleigh Gallichan (11)
Court De Wyck Primary School, Claverham

The Spooky Train

The train goes fast like a flash of lightning
But the people think it is very, very frightening.

The train contains monsters and terrible spiders
But people think they are very good hiders.

The spiders crawl from left to right
But the train sets off in the dead of night.

You think people are going to hide
But someone was dead and his name was Clive.

Thomas Mitchell (8)
Crockerne CE (VC) Primary School, Pill

The Little Bluebird

The little bluebird up in the tree
Hopping around and flying free.
Making nests by collecting twigs
And other things like strings from wigs.
The mother bluebird lays three eggs
While the daddy bluebird collects grasshopper legs.
Very soon the eggs will hatch
I'm telling the truth, the whole batch.
They'll fly away to find a mate
And the parent will go on a holiday date.
The little bluebird has many days
Until he comes to waste away.
Even though Heaven is bliss
His family he did miss.

Lili Harvey (8)
Crockerne CE (VC) Primary School, Pill

Fossils

F ossils are cool
O n them are patterns
S ome are black
S ome are white
I love fossils
L oving fossils is fun.

Francesca May Hollis (7)
Crockerne CE (VC) Primary School, Pill

Holly

H ungry snowmen outside
O ranges being put in stockings
L ight in the sky from a star
L ights being turned on in Pill
Y oyo on the table.

Sophie Hutchings (8)
Crockerne CE (VC) Primary School, Pill

Flowers

Daffodils to roses, bees on the roses,
Bees in the water, they fly away.
Bees going to roses and sucking the honey
From the flowers.
One falls in the water
They fly away.
Bees finding flowers to get some honey,
One broke its wing,
One fell in the water and they flew away.

Ryan Croker (8)
Crockerne CE (VC) Primary School, Pill

The Christmas Holly Poem

H ug Father Christmas or he will cry
O ranges being squeezed by elves
L ights being put up by my mum
L ights being displayed in town
Y oyos for a present.

Tanya Hanlon (8)
Crockerne CE (VC) Primary School, Pill

Flowers

F lowers are pretty.
L avender smells sweet.
O rchids are white and purple.
W allflowers can be yellow and pink.
E delweiss, they are white.
R oses are red.

Lucy Mayer (8)
Crockerne CE (VC) Primary School, Pill

Christmas

C hristmas is coming.
H olly berries are ripe and red.
R eindeer are pulling Santa's sleigh.
I t's the special time of year again.
S pecial carols sung by children.
T oday will be great.
M um and dad will be tired when we wake them up early.
A nything could happen.
S ome day we will be adults and we will be woken up early.

Alexander Leakey (9)
Crockerne CE (VC) Primary School, Pill

Fairies

Fairies, fairies, dancing on Sundays.
They're not big at all, but they are very small.
They can fly very fast, like a balloon flying past.
They like flowers and playing with their powers.
Some are good and some are bad,
I think good fairies are glad.

Megan Birch Morgan (9)
Crockerne CE (VC) Primary School, Pill

Snow

S inging children, singing carols
N ow everyone is having hot drinks
O pening presents under the tree
W hat are other people thinking today?

Eloise Wheeler (8)
Crockerne CE (VC) Primary School, Pill

Lucy Lamb

Lucy was born one day in May
A little lamb, she loved to play
She tried to climb a tree quite high
She wanted to see if she could fly.

She loved to play with all her friends
Five very small black hens
They jumped about and slid around
They all kept falling on the ground.

One day Lucy's mother said
Sorry dear, your father's dead
Lucy cried for days on end
Then she found a brand new friend.

Her new friend was Billy Bear
He was old and had no hair
Lucy loved him with all her heart
And swore that they would never part.

Natasha Brooks (11)
Crockerne CE (VC) Primary School, Pill

When I Grow Up I Want To Be . . .

Something out of the ordinary
Not a builder, not a baker
Not a cook or undertaker

When I grow up I want to be
The very best that I can be
I'm not quite sure, I'll wait and see
Right here right now I want to be
Me!

Jack Sharp (10)
Crockerne CE (VC) Primary School, Pill

In The School Yesterday

In the school yesterday
Everyone was manic
Because Mrs Ross was in
A great big panic.

In the school yesterday
Everything was quiet
All the children came out to play
Suddenly it was a riot.

In the school yesterday
At lunch time
All of us were eating
While doing our rhymes.

In the school yesterday
Home time is near
We all have to listen
Very well, my dear.

In the school yesterday
Home time is here
We all jump for joy
While we do our cheer.

In the school yesterday
Everyone was manic
Because Mrs Ross was
In a great big panic.

Phoebe Sherborne (10)
Crockerne CE (VC) Primary School, Pill

Half Term

School has broken up
Time to have fun
Revision on hold
Let's hope there's some sun.

Pack the car
We are on our way
Let's hope there's no traffic
And we don't delay.

It's late in the day
And we have all checked in
I'm hot and sweaty
So off for a swim.

Tired and grumpy
It's time for bed
Tomorrow's another day
I can't think ahead.

What a brilliant week
We've had such a great time
Now it's all over
And I have to make a rhyme.

Half term finished
Lots of fun I've had
Homework completed
I'm so glad!

Jack Parslow (10)
Crockerne CE (VC) Primary School, Pill

The School Bus

Quick, quick, get on the bus,
Hurry up, we're in a rush,
Put on your belt, grab a seat,
Oh no, the door's shut on Pete!

Off we go, slowly along,
Are you alright, is anything wrong?
Oh dear, the road ahead is blocked,
We might not get there till 10 o'clock.

Everyone cheer, we are nearly there,
Hey you, get back on your chair.
Oh dear, we will have to turn around,
Pete's left his lunch down on the ground.

Grace Arnall (11)
Crockerne CE (VC) Primary School, Pill

Angus' Number Poem

1 a tall and funny man
2 a guy who is getting a tan
3 someone from a story tale
4 a guy who is drinking ale
5 a guy who came from the dead
6 a guy with a really big head
7 a man with a moustache and beard
8 that man is extremely weird
9 a man who is really bright
10 a guy who is out of sight.

Angus Mason (7)
Crockerne CE (VC) Primary School, Pill

Everyday

School sucks
life's great
having fun playing with mates
staying home
annoying sister
bit her finger
gave her a blister
fighting dad
for remote
bit his thumb
stepped on his toe
pinched his nose
dad howls
walk in kitchen
mum scowls
sent to room
want to play
life is like
this, everyday!

James Smith (11)
Crockerne CE (VC) Primary School, Pill

Spring Is Great

S pring is before summer,
P retty flowers are seen,
R inging bells say spring is here,
I ce is gone,
N ight comes and it is warmer,
G rass is growing.

Bethany Taylor (9)
Crockerne CE (VC) Primary School, Pill

Please Mrs Ross

Please Mrs Ross
Can I write the date?
I haven't messed around today
Or been late.

I hung up my coat
For the first time in years
Now if I could just write the date
I wouldn't have to suffer my fears.

Now I've written the date
I'll be ready to start
Now my pen isn't working
I'll have to take it apart.

Rosey Skilbeck (10
Crockerne CE (VC) Primary School, Pill

I'm A Cat

Pull my tail
Scratch my ears
I told mum
It will end in tears

I'm smaller than my siblings
They pick on me lots
They call me names
And nicknamed me 'Tots'

But then I save
My sister's life
My brother helps
They love me alright.

Connie Mansfield (10)
Crockerne CE (VC) Primary School, Pill

Supply Teachers

Supply teachers
Dirty and mean
They never clean
Never come as a team
And they're always eating baked beans.
They take our toys
Telling off the girls and boys
And always making a great big noise.
They send us to the Head
They look like they're dead
And they never go to bed.

They're dirty and mean
They never clean
Never compete as a team
And they're always eating baked beans.

Jay Webber-Andrews (10)
Crockerne CE (VC) Primary School, Pill

Please Miss G

Please Miss G, can I tidy the class?
No you cannot, you tidied it last.
It's Emma's turn today,
We have to be fair,
Now run along Alice
Go over there.

Will someone take the laptop?
Alice, your hand shot up first,
Why don't you go with Georgia,
Before you burst.

Emma Gould (9)
Crockerne CE (VC) Primary School, Pill

My New School

Today I started at
my new school
some kids were kind
and some kids were cruel

next I went into
the girls' bathroom
and to my surprise
I met someone I knew

She showed me
round and round
I didn't make
any sound.

She told me there
were loads of things
she'd tell me
if I gave her a ring

Today I started at
my new school
some kids were kind
and some kids were cruel.

Robyn Byrne (9)
Crockerne CE (VC) Primary School, Pill

The School Poem

It was early in the morning
Walking into school
Everyone was working
My class were in the pool

They were running outside
Into the playground
People playing football
I was running round

It was golden time
I was having fun
So was everyone else
Playing in the sun

Now it's home time
I've got my lunch box
Everyone is walking home
I even saw a fox

I was doing homework
It was RE
Then I went outside
To do some PE.

Oliver James Gedge (9)
Crockerne CE (VC) Primary School, Pill

Dinner Hall

They line up for their dinner
Like little angels in the sky
Look, the teacher's gone
They live most of their lives a lie

They're really little devils
Five, four, three, two, one
Argh! Oh no, here they come
Chucking all their lovely buns
Chewing ugly gum

The children are ecstatic
Running in and out of the class
Bring out the school equipment
The cook just couldn't last

The head teacher hears all the racket
She wonders what it is
The kids are having a food fight
Chucking food at Mrs Ross
The head teacher puts a stop to it
Oh no, here comes her boss!

Ava Parry (9)
Crockerne CE (VC) Primary School, Pill

The Disco Dilemma

The school disco we had yesterday
Was quite a big dilemma.
Everyone was tap dancing
Under Miss Kylema.

Miss Kylema in a fluster
Is not a pretty sight.
The flashing lights were way too bright,
So she fainted in the night.

Everybody cheered then,
For now they would be free at last.
Oh!
We will have a blast!

The school disco we had yesterday
Was quite a big dilemma.
Everyone was tap dancing
Under Miss Kylema.

Sophie Cashman (10)
Crockerne CE (VC) Primary School, Pill

Voices

One day at school there were -
boys screaming
girls shouting
teachers moaning
dogs howling

bombs dropping
birds singing
frogs burping
woodlice chewing
squirrels jumping

Nearly the end of the day
kids jumping
teachers cheering with joy.

Jake Mobbs (10)
Crockerne CE (VC) Primary School, Pill

Tim, The Clumsy Cowboy

He shoots everybody in sight,
Even at night.
He sees many slithering snakes,
He loves to bake desert cakes.
His gun is as big as pencil,
He has a horse that's slow as a snail.
He has got a useless son who is eleven,
Tim is thirty seven.
Tim once shot a sparrow,
With a bow and arrow.
He loves to eat pies,
Which have heaps of flies.
Fast horses and lassoes are not for him
The clumsy cowboy, Tim.

Tom Bullen (7)
Horsington CE Primary School, Horsington

Fantasy Fairies

Fantasy fairies as small as bluebells,
Glittery wings shine in the moonlight,
With a sparkle in their eyes,
Glistening gowns,
Fit for a twilight ball.
Tiny, shiny shoes twinkle,
With each dainty step.
Gorgeous as a lily,
Stunning as a snowdrop.
Gleaming tiaras,
Sprinkling fairy dust
Whilst they spin.
Beautiful butterflies carry them home,
With a beat of their wings.
Apples for their carriages,
Green and scarlet.
Violets and poppies are their homes,
Stumbling to bed,
Hear their petite snores
As they drift off to sleep.

Katy Rumbelow (9)
Horsington CE Primary School, Horsington

Creepy Crocodile

The ferocious crocodile
Slides in the slimy swamp.
Green as grass,
With a sly eye like a fox
Which is as shiny as a sparkly star.
Skin as hard as rock
And teeth as sharp as a knife,
It splashes like a dolphin.

Phoebe Morris (7)
Horsington CE Primary School, Horsington

Pirate Expedition

Captain Jack orders the sails
to be hoisted, like a bullet.
Captain Jack sidles down to the damp and dark hold,
Lurking in the darkness is something, watching.
Bang!
Suddenly, a piercing scream,
Captain Jack hurtled up to the deck,
Crew lying dead and dying
is the sight he witnessed.
Bang!
Captain Jack lay dead.
All are dead!
Killed by villainous pirates.

Matthew Salthouse (9)
Horsington CE Primary School, Horsington

Funky Fairies

Funky fairies fly
Through the night sky,
Sparkling, shimmering wings
and shiny, silver shoes.
Glittering gowns of many colours.

Magical mayhem,
Casting spells,
Twinkling tiaras,
Shimmering in the moonlight.

Fabulous fashion,
with fragile toes,
beautifully attractive
and as tiny as bluebells.

Jessica Brewer (8)
Horsington CE Primary School, Horsington

Felicity, The Kind Fairy

A kindly fairy appeared from under the tall, damp grass.
Her cheeks as red as a rose,
Wearing a tiny, blue dress,
Minute wings and golden hair,
Flying past a muddy and wet marsh
To the multicoloured meadow.
Landing on a beautiful poppy
With its delicate, green stem.
Felicity lives in a country garden, in a dark city.
She magically removes mess!

Ellie Martin (9)
Horsington CE Primary School, Horsington

Crocodile

Crunching crocodile
with sharp teeth,
Scaly skin
gnarled with age,
Ancient grin
with scary smile,
Long, spiky tail
wiggling in the damp earth,
Quietly moving
through the black water,
Glaring eyes
watching and waiting!

Olivia Wingate (7)
Horsington CE Primary School, Horsington

The Dream Fairies

Dream fairies are as tiny as flower buds,
Watching you stagger up to your bed.

Tiny fairies with fine fingers
Create hovering globes of magic
Which enter your dreams,
Making marvellous magic and cheerful dreams.

Dream fairies, making your slumbers sweet,
Flying as fast as lightning, just for you,
Grand, glorious dream fairies!

Sophie Maunsell (8)
Horsington CE Primary School, Horsington

Fairies

Living in the treetops,
Safe in their skyscraper,
Using what they've found around them,
To make their pots and pans.
Leaves for plates,
Petals for blankets,
Flowers for their pillows,
Silk for their trousers,
Bluebells for their hats,
Buttercups for the tops
And leaves for their frocks.
Bark for their table,
Twigs for table legs and chairs,
Cups made from acorns,
Daffodils and sunflowers for their chairs.
Oh, how I wish to be a fairy,
As magical as can be.

Rebecca Croxton (8)
Horsington CE Primary School, Horsington

The Destroyer Crock

Boom! rolled the dark water,
Flesh-eating
Fire-breathing
Black as a space destroyer.
Crocodile rolled over and over,
Dragging itself and coming ashore,
Other people ran to safety.

Swallowing its prey,
As other animals run in horror,
Slipping back into the shocking deep,
It hides, waiting.
As green as the forest
Which surrounds the water.
Everything scared to move!

James Dighton (7)
Horsington CE Primary School, Horsington

Cowboys

Cowboys are quick,
Riding their precious horses,
As fast as speeding bullets,
So they can escape their enemies.
Stetson hats and fringed jackets,
Handkerchiefs over their faces.
Holsters, holding gleaming guns,
Boots with spiky spurs,
Fighting Indian tribes
Or stealing money from banks!

Alfie Jones (8)
Horsington CE Primary School, Horsington

Magical Mermaids

Magical mermaids,
swim in the deep, blue sea.
glide through the sparkling water,
as happy as can be.
Play with delightful fish.
Brushing their shiny hair,
With a little song.

Mermaids swim.
As fast as a silver grey shark.
With their shiny tails,
They never play in the dark.
Mermaids love their golden, long hair,
Their skin as smooth as a pebble.
But don't go near the pirates,
So *beware!*

Alice Jackson (9)
Horsington CE Primary School, Horsington

Cowboys Vs Indians

Indians, riding horses bareback,
Cowboys, on saddles,
Thundering like tanks,
Galloping across the banks,
Cowboy hats and glittering guns,
Bullets and arrows flying through the air,
To attack their enemies.

Toby Crabb (8)
Horsington CE Primary School, Horsington

Mermaid World

Mermaids are very adventurous,
Hair as silky as embroidery thread,
Mermaids sleeping in the sun,
Swimming like dolphins,
Kind and beautiful.

Tails shining in the sun,
As scaly as crocodiles.
Mermaids smell of salty sea
Swimming in the sea with the turtles,
Each one different from the other.

Sitting on the slipper rocks,
Listening to the pounding waves.
How many times have they sent sailors to their graves?

Siobhán Reynolds (8)
Horsington CE Primary School, Horsington

Fluttering Fairies

Wearing green leaf dresses,
Wings are as silky as a sheet,
Eyes are as shiny as diamonds,
Hair is as blonde as gold,
Feet are as tiny as a bottle top,
Glowing like the full moon,
Head as petite as a pearl,
Helping to save magic.
But if we don't believe
It could be tragic!

Amelia Tarling (8)
Horsington CE Primary School, Horsington

Crocodile In The Swamp

A dark, creepy reptile living in the bubbling swamp,
Slimy skin and teeth as sharp as a knife.
One eye watching everything,
Nasty as a bully.
He has a tail with spikes on,
Green as a tree.
Watching for a fish to swim by,
With a *snap!* Of its jaws
The fish is just a memory
In the crocodile's eye!

Alice Liddle (7)
Horsington CE Primary School, Horsington

Fabulous Fairies

As pretty as flowers,
Fluttering in the clouds,
As gentle as a lamb,
Dresses made from nature,
Sparkling shoes from a spider's web.
Hearing whispers in the trees,
Flying in a windy breeze,
Eyes are as green as a leaf,
Some pretty, some disagreeable,
Some think they're superior,
But all are marvellous.

Kate Homer (9)
Horsington CE Primary School, Horsington

Cowboys And Their Horses

Cowboys, riding fast on their horses,
Like the wind.
Shooting guns,
Pistols blazing,
In the blazing sun.
Chasing buffalo,
Using their lassoes.
Camping out in the howling wind.
Dancing wild horse
Bucking and reeling.
Stetson and spurs.

Megan Terry (8)
Horsington CE Primary School, Horsington

Fairy

Fairies hide in beautiful buttercups,
As small as diamonds,
Glinting in the sun,
Sprinkling magic fairy dust
Wearing sparkling party dresses
And shiny crowns.
Fairies, as quiet as a leaf
Falling to the ground.
Perfume on their wings,
Wands that bring magic
And carry away my teeth.

Jasmine Hooper (8)
Horsington CE Primary School, Horsington

Delicate Fairy

The delicate fairy flies to the magical rose.
Purple petals as smooth as marble.
Carrying a bag made of silver leaves,
Collecting magical dust from flowers.
Wearing a pearly pink dress,
Perfect for a twinkling party.
As tiny as a delightful bead.
Making tinkling sounds, like a bell,
Seeing things invisible to humans,
Smelling like honeysuckle.
Living in the treetops,
In a pile of leaves!

Francesca Wagstaff (8)
Horsington CE Primary School, Horsington

Pirates

Fiery pirates protect
Their treasure from their enemies.
Gigantic ships
With sails, cannons and sailors.
Some are cunning and some clumsy,
Missing eyes with patches,
Missing legs with pegs,
Missing hands with hooks.
Captains' calling the orders,
Crew climbing the rigging,
All fearing Jolly Roger.

Beware of *pirates!*

Sián Charlotte Reynolds (8)
Horsington CE Primary School, Horsington

Screaming Pirate

Screaming pirate
With dazzling parrot,
Wooden galleon
With white sails.

Swab the decks,
Climb the rigging,
Hoist the Jolly Roger,
Smiling skull.

With crossed bones,
Scared victims killed
By villain's knives,
Daggers and swords.

Swishing through the air,
Treasure chest marked
On a map
With a red cross.

Gold coins and precious necklaces,
Hidden on a sandy island,
Underground.

Harry Carnell (9)
Horsington CE Primary School, Horsington

I Am Scared Of A Fox

I am scared of a fox
Like a house is terrified of a demolition ball,
Like cats are scared of dogs,
Like a pheasant is terrified of a hunter,
Like people are scared of a machine-gun,
Like a toy is scared of a bin.
I am scared of a fox.

Daniel Powney (10)
Kilmersdon CE (VA) Primary School, Kilmersdon

I Am Scared Of Heights

I am scared of heights
Like a log is horrified by a chainsaw,
Like a cat is scared of a dog,
Like a piece of cheese is scared of a grater,
Like shoes are scared of feet,
Like a pencil is terrified of a sharpener,
Like a car is afraid of a crusher,
Like a bed is afraid of a person,
Like food is scared of a mouth.
I am scared of heights.

Millie Bishop (8)
Kilmersdon CE (VA) Primary School, Kilmersdon

I Am Scared Of Heights

I am scared of heights
Like a necklace is scared of a neck,
Like a chair is scared of a bottom,
Like a bed is terrified of a person,
Like a door is afraid of a door handle,
Like a hairband is scared of hair.
I am scared of heights.

Rachel Ayles (9)
Kilmersdon CE (VA) Primary School, Kilmersdon

I Am Scared Of Mice

I am scared of mice
Like a fish is scared of a pike,
Like a chick is terrified of a fox,
Like the sun is nervous of the clouds,
Like a sweet is terrified of a wrapper,
Like a shark is scared of a sea monster.
I am scared of mice.

Faris Ravetta (8)
Kilmersdon CE (VA) Primary School, Kilmersdon

One

I met a large red dragon
In a dark, cold, damp, misty cave.
It had huge red scales,
Dark piercing eyes.
Gigantic ripped wings
And sharp, silky, curved teeth!
The dragon bellowed, 'Come to my dinner with me, we are having
                                            meat and bone!'
'No!' I screamed! 'I will not let you have me for dinner!'
That is who I met yesterday.

Regan Downing (9)
Kilmersdon CE (VA) Primary School, Kilmersdon

I Am Scared Of Ghosts

I am scared of ghosts
Like a fly is scared of a flytrap,
Like a hedge is scared of a hedge trimmer,
Like a sheep is scared of the shears,
Like a box is scared of fire,
Like a tree is scared of a chainsaw.
I am scared of ghosts.

Ben Watts-Hewson (10)
Kilmersdon CE (VA) Primary School, Kilmersdon

I Am Scared Of Churches

I am scared of churches at night
Like a pig is afraid of a butcher,
Like a fire is scared of water,
Like a rabbit is anxious of a gun,
Like hair is horrified of the hairdresser,
Like hands are terrified of stinging nettles.
I am scared of churches at night.

Sam Watts (8)
Kilmersdon CE (VA) Primary School, Kilmersdon

One

I met a gnome, as content as can be in a forest by a lake.
He was holding a fishing rod and whistling a tune,
The jolly little thing was wearing a waistcoat with a spotty bow tie
And a red Father Christmas hat.
I stammered, 'Hello.'
The gnome turned around and bellowed, 'Hello Fatty!'
I turned bright red and bellowed, 'Come back you puny rat!'
But the gnome was too fast, he was gone in a few seconds flat.
This is one of the people I met yesterday.

Emily Boyd-Nash (9)
Kilmersdon CE (VA) Primary School, Kilmersdon

I Am Scared Of Heights

I am scared of heights
Like a bath is petrified of water,
Like a piece of paper is nervous of the shredder,
Like a shoe is scared of a foot,
Like a nail is anxious of nail varnish,
Like a pillow is afraid of a head.
I am scared of heights.

Georgia Pielesz (8)
Kilmersdon CE (VA) Primary School, Kilmersdon

I'm Scared Of Ghosts

I'm scared of ghosts
Like a fish is scared of a frying pan,
Like a target is terrified of a gun,
Like an elephant is anxious about a poacher,
Like a computer is scared of malfunctioning,
Like wood is terrified of fire.
I'm scared of ghosts.

Dexter Brodrick (9)
Kilmersdon CE (VA) Primary School, Kilmersdon

One

I stumbled into an albino werewolf in the dark and gloomy forest,
It had sharp teeth,
It had powerful jaws and legs -
Tail with matted fur,
White as a polar bear.
'*Howwlll, howwlll, howl* to the moon
And I hope to see you doing this soon,' screamed the werewolf.
'I doubt that I could howl like you but I'll try anyway though. *Howwlll!*
Was that OK?'

Jack Parsons (9)
Kilmersdon CE (VA) Primary School, Kilmersdon

One

I met a minute dwarf by the side of the road.
He wore tiny brown shoes,
The smallest jade suit you could imagine,
His small shorts were held up by a pair of grey stockings.
'I'll see you another day,' he smiled in a way.
I smiled in a way and said, 'OK!'
This is one of the people I met yesterday.

Richard Bowker (8)
Kilmersdon CE (VA) Primary School, Kilmersdon

I Am Scared Of Dogs

I am scared of dogs,
Like a robin is anxious of cats,
Like a dog is frightened of wolves,
Like a bee is nervous of a man,
Like a fish is afraid of pikes,
Like a sun is terrified of the moon.
I am scared of dogs.

Bonnie Weeks (10)
Kilmersdon CE (VA) Primary School, Kilmersdon

One

In the distance I saw an unusual horse,
As thin as a dog, as bony as a stick insect.
I crept to a safe distance then started sketching it.
'What are you doing?' he shouted.
'I'm just sketching you,' I replied.
'Get out of my way,' he shrieked.
Angrily I walked away.
This is one of the people I met yesterday.

Billy Seymour (9)
Kilmersdon CE (VA) Primary School, Kilmersdon

One

I saw a small snake
No bigger than a skipping rope,
With scaly skin and sharp fangs,
With a black tongue and amber eyes.
Sssay what is this creature?
'Are you thinking I am food?'
'I am not prey you horrible little nasty stray.'
This is one of the people I met yesterday.

Sebastian Roberts (10)
Kilmersdon CE (VA) Primary School, Kilmersdon

I Am Scared Of A Carp Fish

I am scared of a carp fish
Like a slice of cheese is scared of a knife,
Like the ground is horrified of a spade,
Like a tree is anxious of an axe,
Like an ant is scared of a foot,
Like a horse is freaked by the farrier.
I am scared of a carp fish.

Jacob Williams (9)
Kilmersdon CE (VA) Primary School, Kilmersdon

One

I disturbed a tiger in a dark, gloomy jungle,
With small red eyes to catch small brown mice,
As well as some huge teeth.
'I am the king of dark, gloomy jungle,' he yelled.
I threw a ball of wool
And he chased after it,
So I could run away.
This is one of the people I met yesterday.

Georgia Hughes (8)
Kilmersdon CE (VA) Primary School, Kilmersdon

I Am Scared Of Girls

I am scared of girls,
Like paper is scared of a shredder,
Like grass is scared of a mower,
Like wood is scared of a sander,
Like happiness is scared of evil,
Like dark is scared of light.
I am scared of girls.

Josiah Bond (10)
Kilmersdon CE (VA) Primary School, Kilmersdon

I Am Scared Of Heights

I am scared of heights
Like hair is scared of scissors,
Like a sheep is terrified of the shears,
Like grass is scared of a lawnmower,
Like a house is scared of a bulldozer,
Like a chicken is scared of a fox.
I am scared of heights.

Rowan Read (9)
Kilmersdon CE (VA) Primary School, Kilmersdon

One

I met a miniature gnome
In my big back garden shed.
The gnome was rather horrid
But I prefer kind gnomes instead.
I asked him a question
And this is what he said,
'Hello mortal, my name is Morgrim,
Leader of the Goon tribe.'
'Where is the Goon tribe?' I said.
'In the middle of Hawaii. Bye boy.'
And then he whisked away,
This is one of the people I met yesterday.

Sam Woodruff (9)
Kilmersdon CE (VA) Primary School, Kilmersdon

My Dad And Mum

My dad is tall and strong and sings loads of funny songs
My dad works, plays and stays in bed on Saturdays
My dad's football mad, telly-shouting, sounds so bad
My dad, I love him, he cheers me up when I am sad,
My dad.

My mum, she puts loads of food in my tum
My mum does everything, she cleans, washes and does all the dishes
My mum, she is the best, she makes me feel better when I am stressed
My mum I love so much, she tells me stories, tucks me in, says
                                        goodnight and says God bless
My mum.

Charley Buchan (8)
Oldfield Park Junior School, Bath

Through The Window

Through the window I can see
A field with a park waiting for me.

I am playing on the swings with snow in my hair
Snowflakes are falling down from the air.

The sky is white
My nose is red
I am wrapped up warm
So the snow doesn't get me wet.

The snowflakes are falling thick and fast
I'm getting cold so it's time to go
As . . .

Through the window I can see
A mug of hot cocoa waiting for me.

Brooklyn Ashdown-Doel (8)
Oldfield Park Junior School, Bath

Quit Smoking Today!

If problems are not your thing
Then cigarettes should be put in the bin
It makes pollution
So don't be a nuisance
And quit smoking.

Daniel Clausen (10)
Oldfield Park Junior School, Bath

The Door

I will not open the door,
I shall not open the door,
My dad said, 'The door is forbidden for all creatures.'

But I will not open the door,
But I shall not open the door,
My brother said, 'Go on, open the door.'

I went to open the door,
I opened the door,
But there was only a photo lying there of all of us.

I went through all that to see a photo,
It said on the back 'don't open the next door',
There was a door right next to it.

Maybe that's the door I can't open!

Toby Fielding (10)
Oldfield Park Junior School, Bath

Pancake Making

Wash your hands and have a laugh
Put the butter in a pan
See it bubble like a bath

Now it's ready for the batter
That's the flour, eggs and water
Watch it cooking in the pan

Now it's ready for a toss
Flipping over once or twice
I hope it makes the pan

Now it's nice and brown
Ready for the lemon and sugar
Umm, let's make another.

Tom Matthews (9)
Oldfield Park Junior School, Bath

Primeval

Primeval is the best
It is better than all the rest
The anomalies are freaky
Conner is a bit wet but really quite a sweetie!
From years past to the future ahead
It's really quite scary, will they end up dead?
The sabre-tooth tiger to the large-like alligator,
What will happen next?
I think I'll find out later!
From the giant scorpion to the small centipede,
What will they do and what will they need?
Cutter is a nutter,
Although he is not a boy he is a man
Will he or will he not always have a plan?

Jasmine Jade Knight (8)
Oldfield Park Junior School, Bath

My Football

Oh my football, my football,
I love to shoot it,
But whenever I shoot it
Bang! 'The fence, oh no!'
I broke the fence.
Oh well, my football, my football,
I love to boot it,
But whenever I boot it
It keeps going over the top.
'Oh no! I think I heard it pop.'

Tom Whittaker (9)
Oldfield Park Junior School, Bath

Jack The Cat

There is a cat called jack
Who lives in a village at number twenty-three,
He's such a fat cat
And he likes to wear hats
And he comes home at eight for his tea,
He's blacker than black and he sits on a mat.
This is my cat called Jack.

Evie Hillier (8)
Oldfield Park Junior School, Bath

The Bumblebee

Bumblebee, bumblebee
Sit on the branch.
Bumblebee, bumblebee
Do a little dance.
Bumblebee, bumblebee
Fly to France,
Ow! It stung me!

Maisey Sprake (7)
Oldfield Park Junior School, Bath

Telescope - Haiku

Telescope, that's me.
You can use me at night-time,
Gaze at Mars through me.

Alexis McLeod (10)
Oldfield Park Junior School, Bath

All I Can Think About . . .

All I can think about is Paddy.
He is loving and caring,
As gentle as a butterfly,
He's the cutest puppy in town.

Everyone on our street shouts,
'Look, there's Paddy!'
He's trustworthy and can always be trusted.

Playful and bouncy,
Jumping and barking,
Chasing the cats and digging holes,
Never mind . . .
We love him and he loves us!

Ruthie Marshall (7)
Oldfield Park Junior School, Bath

Walk To School

W alking to school is lots of fun
A ll the boys and girls having fun
L ook at them over there
'K ids are cool,' they cry.

T his is what we do at break time
O n one leg we bounce around!

S hout, 'Let's have a run!
C ome and play with us,
H i ho, we're having fun!'
O n the ground we jump about,
O ver there the kids shout,
L ove walking to school.

Megan Fortune (8)
Oldfield Park Junior School, Bath

The Friendly Window Cleaner

There's a face at the window.
There's a clatter of metal ladders.
There's a sweep of a sponge.
There's a bucket of water.
He's like a fireman going up to a burning block of flats.
There's a clunk of a drawer and a grab of a pen.
My mum writes him a cheque and before I know it,
With the blink of an eye he's gone, gone, gone!

Hamish James Kale (9)
Oldfield Park Junior School, Bath

Down Under The Blue

Stick-like creatures staring into nothingness,
Large, round wooden things bobbing on the water.
Extraordinarily roll along the ground,
Vibrating the water and everything around.

The wailing wind always ringing through my ears,
The murmurs and mutters keeping me awake,
The patter of the feet above
Sounds like the ticking of a clock.

All on my abandoned own, unloved, lost and lonely,
Down-hearted and distraught, scared and unhappy,
I feel like I'm destroyed,
With no one to love me and no one to care.

But sometimes it can be very pleasant down here.
The fish are kind so I'm not always alone.
Above all the bad, there is some good,
The good-ness life can be understood.

Jadene Gardener & Sophie Milsom (11)
Puriton Primary School, Puriton

The Mystery Of The Loch

There, deep in the blue, shining puddle beyond my eyes,
Moving shiny creatures move back and forth in the dark shadows.
A globe of brightness in my eyes,
Stick-like mammals with changing mass.

Mumbling, whispering sounds from up above my good self,
Swishing, swaying and breaking as hard as a heavy beast.
Noisy, clicking flashes above me,
Shrieks of laughter that annoy me.

Lonely, sad, nobody to play with, only the fishes,
Bored, abandoned, still no one to play with, I am glum.
Solitary now and for many eons,
As water passes year to year.

It's not bad being the only one left -
Because everyone crowds around me.

Elspeth Megan MacGeoch & Jordan Palmer (9)
Puriton Primary School, Puriton

Look There's Nessie

There deep in the dark mysterious lake,
I wouldn't make a mistake of trespassing above the sands.
Shadows moving all around like ghosts underground;
Crazy mammals with flashing sounds.

Flashing, shiny gills move quickly through the water,
Gliding past me as I rest so I don't get disturbed.
Murmurs I hear but I can't make out,
The wind is so vicious like enraged lions.

As I feel abandoned by everyone for many years now,
It gets upsetting and scary on my own.
For a long time I have been by myself . . .
I would like some new friends now.

Ellie Lay & Hannah Hughes (10)
Puriton Primary School, Puriton

Loch Ness

Deep inside this gloomy cave,
I heard a thud and crash of the waves,
I went into the blackness,
Nearly at the bottom of Loch Ness.

Spinning blades thundering loudly,
Splishing, splashing children playing,
Crashing waves hit the dangerous rocks,
Thousands of fish come flying by.

Scared and alone my body rots away,
People come to see me which makes me frown,
Angry, but tired, I roar at fish,
I form a feud with tourists passing by.

I am unique, one of a kind,
A real bigshot in my own way,
The leader of my underwater palace,
Fast and agile I glide through the water as king of the loch.

Sam Umimski (10) & Thomas Lonsdale (11)
Puriton Primary School, Puriton

Nessie Of The Loch

Pulsating through the miraculous blue colours,
Writhing with life through and throughout;
Blurs pictures of small things on the crest of the water.
Staring, flashes, temporarily blinding me,
As tall, wiry shapes look uneasily afoot.

Tranquillity broken - forever awake,
Whirring blades and whining murmurs I hear now.
Forever restless, peace has been destroyed,
Never sleeping for all eternity.

Being the last of my kind isn't bad -
By the time I am gone my race shall be extinct.
But when I am dead my heart and my soul
Shall forever and ever stay with my loch.

Asher Bentham (11)
Puriton Primary School, Puriton

Mystery Of The Loch Ness

Here in the deep, blue shadows come through,
Small silvery darts shoot past my eyes.
Clumsy mammals mumble, move talk so much,
Large bellowing pieces of floating junk.

The crashing of waves against rocks,
The noise and screeches travel through.
Swirls in the air coming from bladed birds,
Propellers cluttering my territory.

The wind brushes on my head like snakes,
I'm lonely down here in the blue.
The silver darts brush against my hard scales.
I feel the cold down here in the deep blue.

It's not so bad being the only one,
It's good for me, I get lots of fish.
My species died long ago, I survived,
I'm proud of being the only one.

**Matthew Betteridge, Connor Wolfe-Middleton,
Charlie Attwood & William Lonsdale**
Puriton Primary School, Puriton

Nessie

Water crashing all around her,
The noise of a clicking camera and the echoing coming from
                                                        the surface.
Hear the water splashing all day long
And a roaring as its mystery pops up.

Confused at the loch with no one to play with,
She feels a bit sad and heartbroken
That there is a plesiosaur still alive,
But soon it will be extinct.
More fish, she will watch, hoping one day to get to see
                                                        another plesiosaur,
One day, not so far away.

Melissa Standen & Leah Beechey (10)
Puriton Primary School, Puriton

Down Under The Blue

There in the sapphire, sparkling blue,
Whirling shadows swimming past,
Figures staring down at me,
Darts swimming along the floor,
Glistens without a sound.

Whispers and whistles pass on through
Sounds of the unknown,
Shakes and stirs, crashes and thumps,
Clicking that happens non-stop.

Distress and loneliness fill my heart,
As I wander, looking for a friend,
I feel so full of woe, I feel so low,
Will my life ever end?

Down with the sorrow and up with the joy,
Being on my own is a huge annoy,
But it's not so bad being me,
This might end up happily.

Georgia Edmundson, Leah Turner & Tanisha Birch (11)
Puriton Primary School, Puriton

Loch Ness Mystery

There deep in the true depths of blue flickering shadows,
Transparent, see-through.
Unusual they seem and mysterious,
They will be for all the world,
They shall see.

Echoes and whistles run through the waves,
Swishing and swirling round in the water,
The noises I hear are going through my ears.

The feeling of boredom sweeps across the body,
Sorrow across the heart,
Confusion across the mind.

It's not so bad down here by myself,
Even though I get lonely.
Sometimes the fish come and comfort me,
Oh well - you never know,
This might turn out happily.

Lucy Russell, Melissa Storey, Sophie Hembery & Holly Cartright-Hall
Puriton Primary School, Puriton

Mystery Of The Loch Ness

Masses of blue further than my eyesight,
Flickers of shadows run between my eyes,
Weird they look and silly they seem,
Eyes above the surface, you'll see much more.

Whispers and echoes from the dark abyss,
Swishing waves coming towards me as far as I see,
Silver darts shooting past me to the end
Like ferocious mammals untamed.

I was lonely and distraught when no one knew me,
I was depressed, annoyed and no one would play,
Very unusual and extinct like me,
I need someone to be with me.

But it's not so distressingly bad - being the only one,
So strange although unique in my environment,
Plesiosaurs died except for me,
But not the Loch Ness beast, that is me!

Anthony Lawson-Blake, Liam Chinn, Connor Ferris & Joe Dixon
Puriton Primary School, Puriton

Mystery Of The Loch

There deep in the centre and depths of the blue
Are the shimmers of many shadows throughout.
Above, oval shapes loom over my head,
Bobbing on the surface of the dim blue.

The whispers of the waves echo around
As the gentle current stirs around me.
Whispers and murmurs can be heard from above,
The noise making me unable to sleep in peace.

Puzzled at the land beyond the waters,
I felt lonely to have no companion.
By myself, I felt heavy-hearted,
Downcast, low-spirited, gloomy and dismal.

But it's not bad being one of a kind,
Though plesiosaurs died out long ago.
I can still live in hope that they will come back,
Yet I live happily - Nessie of the loch.

Niamh McKay (11)
Puriton Primary School, Puriton

Mystery Of The Loch

There deep in the outline of the darkness of blue,
Dark, dainty shadows flickered wildly around me,
Large shaped boxes bobbed slowly over the surface,
Stick-like creatures stood around me and peered down at me.

The wailing wind always ringing through my ears,
The murmurs and mutters keeping me awake.
The patter of the feet above
Sounds like the ticking of the clock.

All on my own, abandoned and unloved,
Lost and lonely, downhearted and distraught.
Scared and unhappy, I feel like I'm destroyed,
With no one to love me and no one to care.

It's not so bad being one of a kind,
Though plesiosaurs died out long ago.
I can still live in hope that they will come back,
Yet I live happily, Nessie of the loch.

Amber Howden (10)
Puriton Primary School, Puriton

The Sun

The sun rises slowly,
The silhouetting frisbee,
The stars electricity current kills all,
It is like a golden ball lost over the moonlit seas,
Takes over the torrent of darkness, darkness, darkness,
Takes over the torrent of darkness up to the morning sky.

The sun sprints over the sky,
Eventually now in the noon thigh,
It is now overhead,
No more night sky,
The orangey-yellow colour smacks all it sees,
For the sheer of the colour, colour, colour,
For the sheer of the colour smacks all it sees.

The sun's burning,
Eventually it will die,
It will blow itself to extinction
And from that day it will kill us all, all, all,
And from that day it will kill us all.

Kieran James Woodhouse (10)
Sandford Primary School, Sandford

Fairies And Mermaids!

Fairies have beautiful glittery wings
Mermaids sit on rocks and there they sing
Fairies all have different powers
Mermaids swim under ancient towers
Some lucky fairies deliver the fairy queen's mail
All mermaids have a shining tail
Fairies fly beneath the sun
Mermaids play with the fish and have lots of fun
Fairies are never ever mean
Mermaids are always really keen
Fairies make a lovely rainbow
Mermaids swim very low
Fairies land softly on the ground
Mermaids swim softly all around
Fairies hide in the clouds
Mermaid necklaces are worth a lot of pounds
Fairies have beautiful glittery wings
Mermaids sit on rocks and there they sing.

Jamie O'Connor
Sandford Primary School, Sandford

The Swoop

I look to the creamy red sky to the sight of a bird,
Flying low so not to be heard,
A swoop and a soar,
The rat is no more.
He takes to the sky to fly to his young,
His mysterious call is yet to be sung.

He's like a bomb shooting low,
The farmer with his hoe.
He grabs his gun,
Aims high and pulls the trigger,
The bird is no more, his fate no bigger . . .

But for the young they will be strong,
But still the farmer has done wrong!

Adam Karl Nichols (10)
Sandford Primary School, Sandford

Cars

Cars are big
Cars are small
Cars can be very tall!

Cars are cool
Cars are flash
Cars are worth a lot of cash!

Cars are dirty
Cars are clean
And some can look very mean!

Cars have wheels
Cars have tyres
Cars have lots and lots of wires!

Cars are slow
Cars are fast
And some cars come last!

Gregory Humphry (8)
Sandford Primary School, Sandford

Sea

The full moon glistening over the sea
All the fish were shimmering with glee
Dolphins jumping in the water
And swim about a quarter
The shore whispering up at me
Sand grains blowing and then flee
Smells of ice creams and suntan lotion
Remind me of a happy emotion.

Libby Wilsher-Day (8)
Sandford Primary School, Sandford

Mermaids

Mermaids have tails that shine in the dark
and look at fish that have some marks.
Mermaids have hair that glitters in the sun
and have lots and lots and lots of fun.

Mermaids have many kinds of powers
and stay up for many hours.
Mermaids can swim so deep underwater
floating with the king and daughter.

Mermaids have tails that shine in the dark
and look at fish that have some marks.
Mermaids have hair that glitters in the sun
and have lots and lots and lots of fun.

Mermaids can live forever
and are really, really clever.
Mermaids like to swim with dolphins
and wear lots of beautiful rings.

Mermaids have tails that shine in the dark
and look at fish that have some marks.
Mermaids have hair that glitters in the sun
and have lots and lots and lots of fun.

Megan Pressling (8)
Sandford Primary School, Sandford

Arctic Amethyst

I walk for days, lost in vast, snowy plains.
Blizzards hit my face like rocks
My blood seems to freeze in an instant.
Every step I take makes me grow weaker,
I start to feel this quest is useless.
I gaze into the deathly snowflakes falling to the earth.
I see a glowing light coming from the ground, like a giant torch.
I sprint towards the light source,
My heart starts to race.
I see a wooden room near the light,
I decide to enter.

Inside, there is a twinkle in every corner
And a shine in every crack.
It is in front of me surrounded in glory,
Bringing light into darkness like a purple angel.
I reach out to grab it and feel it with a light touch,
The door locks behind me,
I'm trapped . . .

Dominic Thorne (11)
Sandford Primary School, Sandford

Scaly Fangs

Living behind the shadow of the shady corn,
Hunting, killing until the day is dawn.
Like a rope strongly tied as tight as it can be,
Constricting the foe to the fate of destiny.
Its teeth are daggers stabbing the weak,
The foe's now short life is at its peak.

Its tongue is as wet as the mystical sea,
The mercy that this serpent gives is as small as a pea.
Slithering along the dry and dusty ground,
Eating small and helpless rodents all around.
As the sparkling, bright sun droughts the earth,
This reptile is a natural, deadly killer at birth.
For this is the lifecycle of this snake,
That has green camouflaging scales as big as a flake.

Adam Jones (11)
Sandford Primary School, Sandford

Puppies

Puppies are cute and fluffy, they like to jump around.
Puppies are cute and fluffy, but they're not big hounds.
Puppies are big, puppies are small,
But you can't get a puppy that is tall.
Pug puppies and Yorkie puppies, one is smooth and one is rough,
One is sweet and one is tough.
One is wrinkly,
But both their eyes are just as twinkly!

Holly Bartholomew (9)
Sandford Primary School, Sandford

Puppies

Puppies bounce
Here and there
They may pounce
On a hare.

Puppies need cuddles
Big ones too
They jump in puddles
And play with you!

Puppies like to play
They dig and bark
Happy in the day
Scared in the dark.

Puppies need to sleep
Long ones too
They may peep
And you may see them too!

Greta Guccione (9)
Sandford Primary School, Sandford

Cats

Big cats stalk
Small cats walk

Big cats eat
But only if it's meat

Small cats like milk
Their fur is nice and like silk

Big cats are mean
Small cats lick themselves clean

Fat cats are lazy
But mine is called Daisy.

Matthew Callow (9)
Sandford Primary School, Sandford

Planets

The sun is a giant orange which produces light,
Then the moon comes out late at night.
Mercury, the first planet from the sun,
Covered with dust and stones, it's done.
Venus is full of volcanoes that are dead,
Shrouded in clouds lighter than lead.
Earth, full of oxygen is our home
With sea over which we roam.
Mars is known as the red planet, full of dust
Its extreme winds are coloured rust.
Jupiter is one of the giants of gas,
Hydrogen and helium is its mass.
Saturn is also a gas giant with a colourful ring,
Through the ice the meteors fling.
Neptune is as blue as a summer's sky,
With methane it is very high.
Uranus is a dark, cold place,
All these planets are high up in space.

Chloe James (11)
Sandford Primary School, Sandford

Wizards And Witches

Wizards and witches
Potions and spells
Cackling through the night
Creating magical light.

Wizards and witches
Potions and spells
On brooms flying high
When the morning is nigh.

Wizards and witches
Potions and spells
Known for wearing hats
And grooming their black cats.

Wizards and witches
Potions and spells
Waving their mysterious wands
And saying 'abracadabra' of which they're fond.

Jack Hill (7)
Sandford Primary School, Sandford

The Seaside

The water hugging the glistening, shining shore,
I'm watching with no book bore.
The sun's like a blown up beach ball,
Slowly it suddenly falls.

Sunbathers so okra brown,
The shimmering sun creates a funny frown.
The toddlers jump into bitterly cold sea,
I'm watching in silence but there in front of me is an annoying bee!

The wind picks up the scratchy sand hitting my little legs,
The washing next door is flying off the pegs.
I struggle to wrestle with mighty gales,
And so are the wailing whales.

Now the whistling wind gets calmer,
To eat a powerful piece of Parma.
I think I see a murmuring mermaid,
But too quick the beautiful scene does fade.

It changes to a pink sunset,
Sitting on the wave.

Georgina Staite (10)
Sandford Primary School, Sandford

Seashell

I have a shell
I lift the beautiful
Thing to my ear
All I hear is fantasies . . .

Of glamorous, gleaming
And elegant sea
Creatures, crawling
Wildly in peace . . .

Of people sunbathing
Tranquilly looking up to the
Silent sky above . . .

Seas of leaping dolphins
Dangerous sharks
Colourful fish
Deep below . . .

I have a shell
I lift the beautiful
Thing to my ear
All I hear is fantasies.

Georgia Douglas (8)
Sandford Primary School, Sandford

The Beach

The beach is a big ball of fun,
Fun surfing on the tidal waves,
Waves all come in massive and small,
Small, the seagulls glide across the ocean.
The ocean, a wonderful watery paradise,
Paradise, with mysterious treasure chests never to be found,
Found, rainbows all colourful and bright,
Bright, the bees who get annoyed and give you a bite!
Bite the baguette and sandy crisps,
Crisps, hey all the seagulls are pinching the lot,
Lots of people chasing a tan,
Tan the colour of sunburnt crowds,
Crowds and my mum are now relaxed,
Relaxed people asleep in deckchairs,
Deckchairs abandoned in the wind,
Wind voracious whips the sand,
Sand in the eyes and ears and so . . .
So my family and I are popping downtown!

Amy Lees (9)
Sandford Primary School, Sandford

The Snow

The snow glistens in the sun,
Everyone is having fun.
Snowballs here, snowballs there,
The snow melts in the air.

The snow glistens in the sun,
'Come on kids,' shouts the mum,
'Build a snowman up so high,
Nearly touching the bright blue sky!'

Francesca Farquharson (7)
Sticklands CE (VA) Primary School, Evershot

The Spear

Used for hunting, war and killing
With a wooden handle and metal prong
Somehow you'll be hunted down!

At nightfall when all is dark
It is the time for hunting.
Having dinner with their catch,
It's deer tonight and roast marshmallow!

In a castle living in luxury
But when enemies come, war is certain.
'Attack!' cry the soldiers, throwing spears,
'We're winning chaps, don't fear!'

So now your question's answered,
No more trouble for you.
For spears are used for killing,
Sleek, sharp and long!

Charlie Oldfield (9)
Sticklands CE (VA) Primary School, Evershot

Butterfly

The butterfly is in the cold breeze
Sheltering in the high trees.
Beautiful big butterfly
Flittering, floating butterfly.

The butterfly swoops and glides
And glistens in the sun.
Butterfly swooping in the night,
Butterfly beautiful and bright.

Alice Glover (7)
Sticklands CE (VA) Primary School, Evershot

The Snail

Out from a wall comes a slithery snail,
Leaving a glistening trail.
As the scaly, slow snail
Crawls into a garden
Destroying all the vegetables on his way.

Alice Crocker (8)
Sticklands CE (VA) Primary School, Evershot

The Garden

In the garden
Bright and beautiful.
The green trees,
The buzzing bees,
The butterfly wings
Are colourful things.

At night the owls
Swoop from the trees.
The mice scatter along
The floorboards of the house.

Everybody is sound asleep
In the snug beds.
Not a little peep
Out of any of them.

Hamish Moore (8)
Sticklands CE (VA) Primary School, Evershot

The Colourful Butterfly

The butterfly came shimmering
In the breeze and sun,
Landing on a flower,
Flapping its colourful wings

As the butterfly came glistening,
In the air flapping its wings.
With its colourful wings,
Like a nice shimmering.

As it was landing on the flower,
Flapping its wings over the wall,
Like a nice colourful butterfly
With its beautiful wings

Chloe Diment (7)
Sticklands CE (VA) Primary School, Evershot

Roses In The Garden

Roses, roses all shapes and sizes,
You never know there are lots of surprises.
Red as blood and smooth as silk,
Like a pink glass of milk.

Roses, roses all shapes and sizes,
You never know there's lots of surprises.
White as snow, cold as ice
In the garden smelling nice.

Scout MacPherson (8)
Sticklands CE (VA) Primary School, Evershot

Shimmering Snow

As the shiny snow falls slowly
I can see tiny snowflakes
Falling from high in the clouds.

Soon the snowflakes settle
Very quickly making no noise at all.

The children come out to play in the shiny snow,
Making a snowman out of the shimmering snow.

Tara Newman (8)
Sticklands CE (VA) Primary School, Evershot

Tigers

Deep in the jungle
There are two tigers in a tumble
The tigers are smooth creatures
They have sharp teeth and are mean
The tigers are orange with stripes
Sharp teeth entrap prey which they eat, ripping the meat.

Nathaniel Anstey (8)
Sticklands CE (VA) Primary School, Evershot

The Beautiful Beach

On the big beach
The sand is a creamy peach
And the sea is a sparkly turquoise,
As the glistening sun hits the sea.

There are surfers on the sea
And people jumping for glee.
Everyone is having fun,
In the light of the big bright sun.

Elizabeth Crocker (9)
Sticklands CE (VA) Primary School, Evershot

Rain

Delightful, delicate drips of wet water
Fall from the gutter and onto my shoulder.
It doesn't take much for loads of water to come toppling down.
Some big, some small, some rather tall.
Some fat, some thin, some that swim,
Like perfect little beads.

Theodora Cottrell (7)
Sticklands CE (VA) Primary School, Evershot

Tigers

Deep in the hot dry jungle
There are two tigers in a tumble.
The tigers are smooth and clean,
They have sharp teeth and are very mean.

The tigers scratch with their sharp claws.
They open their mouths
And they bite their prey with their teeth.
They are gentle and kind underneath.

Callum Symes (8)
Sticklands CE (VA) Primary School, Evershot

Dolphin

Down, down, down
In the deep blue sea
There was a dolphin
As happy as can be.

Up, up, up
In the deep blue sea
Swims the silky dolphin
Coming to see me!

Ellie Robins (8)
Sticklands CE (VA) Primary School, Evershot

School Is Fun

School is full of lots of noise,
Clever girls and naughty boys.
Big and scary it can be
For everyone including me

The teacher is coming, let's all hide,
In the classes and also outside.
The teacher yells, 'Where are you?'
Out they jump and all say, 'Boo!'

Samie Gough (9)
Sticklands CE (VA) Primary School, Evershot

Tiger

Deep in the hot day sun
There are tigers in a tumble.
The tigers are smooth and clean,
They have sharp teeth and are very mean.

The tigers scratch with their mouths
And give a big roar.
They bite their prey with their sharp, shiny teeth.
They rip and shred meat.

Rebecca Glover (7)
Sticklands CE (VA) Primary School, Evershot

Monkeys

Monkeys swing from tree to tree,
Eating big brown bananas on their way.
Smelly monkeys don't put their deodorant on.
Monkeys go to sleep in their big nice den.

Toby Dolan (8)
Sticklands CE (VA) Primary School, Evershot

The Butterfly

As the butterfly swoops, glides and glistens,
In the air there are tons of shapes in flare.
Watch and you will see the amazing butterfly.

The butterfly gracefully glides
And glistens.
In the air it shelters in the trees.
Watch and you will see
The amazing butterfly.

Alexandra Adams (8)
Sticklands CE (VA) Primary School, Evershot

The Shiny Sun

As the sun glistens and glows
I start to think about home.
The sun is a big silvery ball.

Soon the sun is starting to fall.
I feel the warmth fading behind me.
As I walk on I leave the smooth, silvery, shiny sun,
For another day, I will come.

Isobel Farquharson (9)
Sticklands CE (VA) Primary School, Evershot

The Sparkly Snow

The snow falls lightly onto the ground,
Making no sound as it settles.
It glistens and sparkles in the sun
While the children play.

There's snowball fights
And hot cocoa is being warmed.
There are skiers gliding past
And snowboarders going even faster.

Lola Francis (9)
Sticklands CE (VA) Primary School, Evershot

The Golden Flower

The flower so tall,
It's bigger than a ball.
It glows in the sun
Like a hot cross bun.

Its petals unfold,
So beautiful and gold.
Its stem so green,
Darker than a stream.

Its leaves so clean,
Bigger and more beautiful than a bean.
That's all you need to know,
So let her grow.

Esme Diment (9)
Sticklands CE (VA) Primary School, Evershot

My School

Sticklands School is lots of fun,
Here and there you may not run.
There's loads of stuff to do and seek,
So hold your breath and take a peek.

The teachers are hushing boys,
'Listen now, 'No more noise!'
The girls are giggling all day,
'Come now, let's go and play!'

Eilah Berlow (9)
Sticklands CE (VA) Primary School, Evershot

The Sand

The sand is very inviting
The sand is very sweet
The sand is very tickly
Especially on your feet.

The sand is cool and shiny
The sand is lumpy and dry
Swarming around your feet
Like a fluttering butterfly.

I think you ought to know now
That sand is so, so cool
And I think you ought to know
That sand does really rule.

Adam Harris (8)
Sticklands CE (VA) Primary School, Evershot

Tigers

Deep in the hot dry jungle
There are two tigers in a tumble.
The tigers are smooth and clean,
They have shiny teeth and are very mean.

The tigers scratch with their teeth.
They open their mouths.
They bite their prey with their teeth.
They are gentle and kind underneath.

Corey Brimble (7)
Sticklands CE (VA) Primary School, Evershot

Sand

Sand is shimmering,
Sand is shiny,
Sand is silky.
Swimming softly near the sea,
You should go there
And you will find small and big shells.

Jack Ruston (7)
Sticklands CE (VA) Primary School, Evershot

The Sea

The sea is shimmering in the sun,
What can be done?

The sea is shiny and bright at night
And the dolphins are feeling very happy.

The sea is shiny indeed.
As the fish bow to the seaweed.

Imogen Bellfield (7)
Sticklands CE (VA) Primary School, Evershot

Yellow

Shifty, soft sand moving swiftly by the sea.
Soft, downy chick sounding very happy.
Glinting, blinding sun shining so brightly.
Shiny, bright, amber lights telling cars to take the brake off.
Comfy golden chairs standing under the table.
Teacher's amber folder holding all her papers.
Silky, soft cushions which are for the queen.

Melanie Russon (8)
Woolavington Village Primary School, Woolavington

Red

Rosy, metal postbox standing on the noisy street,
Glinting, scarlet skirt lying on the cuddly bed,
Cherry, wooden tables sitting on the wooden floor,
Crinkly, russet books lying on the dusty shelves,
Soft, velvety lips talking to a nice friend,
Wiggly, woggly tongue moving in the cold air,
Hard cardboard boxes stacked on top of each other,
Electric, crimson clock ticks every minute,
Five red crayons sitting in the dirty box,
Sandy, bright light shining so bright,
Squishy round balls bouncing in the hot air,
Hard bumpy house standing on the green hill.

Abbie Fisher (8)
Woolavington Village Primary School, Woolavington

Red

Beautiful gleaming heart beating in my body.
Dark, soft roses swaying in the fresh breeze.
Sun shining postbox gleaming in our eyes.
Soft, light and dark English books in the marking tray.
Juicy, delicious cherries that are in my mouth.

Tom Kidner (8)
Woolavington Village Primary School, Woolavington

Yellow

Bright circular melon with delicious juice.
Shiny bright sun in the dazzling sky.
Amber chunky cheese with yummy crackers.
Chubby hard books with hard words.
Golden curly wallpaper and lovely princesses.
Smooth yet bumpy pencil case like rough bricks.

Chloe Louise Chick (7)
Woolavington Village Primary School, Woolavington

Henry VIII And His Wives

Henry VIII had many wives,
Old and new.
Sporty like a lion and handsome too.
His first wife was Catherine of Aragon
But she was divorced as fast as a paragon.
Next came beautiful Anne Boleyn,
She was not divorced but beheaded.
Her head rolled down the road and stayed all night,
It gave the people a terrible fright.
Then Jane Seymour she died in childbirth,
But Henry got what he needed, a baby boy.
Next he married Anne of Cleeves, but bye-bye Anne,
Next minute she was divorced as fast as a horse.
Next Katherine Howard, only 19, while Henry was 49,
She was beheaded for adultery, poor, poor Katherine.
Lastly Catherine Parr, she survived but Henry died.

Katie Goldrich (9)
Woolavington Village Primary School, Woolavington

Red

A shirt covered in flowers.
A brand new astonishing car filled with diesel.
A bumpy pale roof of polished slate.
A fluffy turquoise carpet in our dining room.
Grey-blue football boots trying to steal the ball.
A feathery hat, smart on a lady.

Kieran Long (8)
Woolavington Village Primary School, Woolavington

Red

Red silky shirt sitting in a wooden wardrobe.
Hard pine tables sitting in a brick room.
Colourful paper books lying on the high shelf.
Rosy metal post box sitting in the front yard.
Cheery crimson lips eating scrumptious food.
Amber slimy tongues licking their crimson lips.
Half plastic clock ticking by itself.
Brick-red crayons colouring by fast hand.
Scarlet crimson house sitting in a big estate.
Cherry-red folder lying on a wooden desk.
Red ripped English books sitting on a scarlet shelf
Red crimson bowls smashed in the box.
Red crimson bows smashed in the plastic.
Bright, bright light protected by the lovely shade.
Red bright Santa's clothes on the way to brick-red houses.

Jack Willis (8)
Woolavington Village Primary School, Woolavington

The Footballer

My dad is just like Wayne.
My dad has power shots the same.
My dad is a great goalie and Rooney is not.
My dad has high shots like Rooney has got
And they both score goals a heck of a lot!

Joshua Foale (8)
Woolavington Village Primary School, Woolavington

The Doctor

Who is the time traveller?
It is the 'doc'.
He travels through time
But I cannot.

Who defeats his evil foe?
It is the 'doc'.
He outwits them all
But I cannot.

Who can get companions?
It is the 'doc'.
He loses them all
But I cannot.

Who is in the TARDIS?
It is the 'doc'.
He travels through time
But I cannot.

Thomas Puddy (9)
Woolavington Village Primary School, Woolavington

The School Zoo

The school is a zoo,
Stampede out of class,
A load of lions going to get fed,
Clank up the stairs,
Huge giant bars,
Running like a monkey up a tree,
But then, when they line up,
They get tamed again.

Jaime Farrell (9)
Woolavington Village Primary School, Woolavington

The Water Park

The water park is just like a penguin,
Black and white.

They splash their feet in the water
And dance swiftly to the people.
They eat the fish from the water
And dive as fast as possible.

The water is clear as a diamond,
You can see all the colourful fish
But then they're gone
In the penguin's tum-tum.

Katie Crossman (9)
Woolavington Village Primary School, Woolavington

The Wave

The wave is a water ride,
If you were it you'd be full of pride,
It waves on the sandy seashore
And it has still got a lot more!
The wave is clashing,
The glass is smashing,
When somebody drops it in,
But no one puts the glass in the silver bin!
I ride on the azure sea,
But no one dares to,
It's just me!
The wave is a water mountain,
Just like a fizzy fountain!

Emma Howes (8)
Woolavington Village Primary School, Woolavington

The Cheetah

A Lamborghini is a speeding cheetah,
Fast and ferocious.
Its streamlined body making it look delicious.
The cheetah has the custard colour of the Lamborghini
But just with chocolate chips.
The doors flip up and inside you will find a chocolate dip.
The sun shines brightly on the eyes of the cheetah.
The Lamborghini speeding down the road getting no weaker.

Charly Moore (9)
Woolavington Village Primary School, Woolavington

Gold

Glinting ring shining in a dusty window
Glinting earring hanging from someone's ear
Shiny dull necklace dangling from someone's neck
Gleaming glistening crayon lying on the floor
Polished cars whizzing down the busy road
Circular money on the window sill
Cubed shaped trophies on a box.

Lucy Pacey (8)
Woolavington Village Primary School, Woolavington

My School Is A Jungle

My school is a jungle. There's no doubt about it,
I am, I am sure.
The teachers shout like elephants that have seen
a mouse in a door!
The head-teacher lion is roaring
But all the young monkeys are snoring.

I am playing catch the deer and the
Bear is chasing me.
I run away to live for the day,
So the bear's got nothing for tea.

See I told you it is a jungle
So . . .
Watch out for the bear
Because he might catch you!

Caitlin Pinney (9)
Woolavington Village Primary School, Woolavington

Aston Martin And The Snake

Aston Martin is a sleek snake,
Reacts as fast as a flicking tongue
That goes for its prey.
It snakes across the mountain roads
Roaring and snarling as it goes.

Samuel Bate (8)
Woolavington Village Primary School, Woolavington

Red

The giant red post box opened by the postman
A glittering rosy box getting pulled off the shelf
Chunky, beautiful, red folders put on the shelf
Juicy falling tomatoes splatting on the ground
Lovely little scarlet tiles falling off the humongous house
Huge heavy dragon fruit flying from the Caribbean
Nice scarlet apple munched in a little boy's mouth
One ruby English book on the wooden shelves
Brand new red smiley face, full in five days
Special clean red table arriving from Argos
Wobbly bean bags sitting on the hall floor.

Henry Isaacs (8)
Woolavington Village Primary School, Woolavington

The School Playground

The school playground is a cauldron of soup,
Multicoloured and moving.
It simmers at first,
With its foamy surfaces and bubbling depth.
The cauldron is spitting and gurgling, getting hotter and hotter,
Like children boiling.

Kayla Rossiter (8)
Woolavington Village Primary School, Woolavington

Young Writers Information

We hope you have enjoyed reading this book - and that you will continue to enjoy it in the coming years.

If you like reading and writing poetry drop us a line, or give us a call, and we'll send you a free information pack.

Alternatively if you would like to order further copies of this book or any of our other titles, then please give us a call or log onto our website at www.youngwriters.co.uk

**Young Writers Information
Remus House
Coltsfoot Drive
Peterborough
PE2 9JX
(01733) 890066**